Readers' Comments

"RDS is truly a bold and daring total company approach to customer management and long term relationship building. RDS opens and clarifies communication, relationship (customer and internal), and a new understanding on internal capability. If the intent of this book is to get someone to look seriously at change, this book hits a home run."

Terry Haverkost, Retired Director, PepsiCo

"RDS is compelling. Different. Meaningful. Contemporary. RDS takes the real concept that buyers buy, sellers don't sell anymore into action and the approach is truly valuable. Negative Planning and Knowledge Quest are not intuitive and therefore will stick with you long after you finish reading."

James Mock, Midwest Financial Staffing LLC

"Selling Without Salespeople is surely a no holds barred book. The references to former clients and individuals were straight to the point. Being involved in business and politics for years, I find this approach very different and refreshing."

Robert Priselac, Technology Consultant, Government Relations

"After several decades in sales and managing customer relationships, I couldn't help but think how much more successful we could have been had we fully utilized the resources around us. If you are in any sales role, take a hard look at your current situation and get involved in RDS if your company is fortunate enough to have the vision to embrace this philosophy."

Bob Daniels, Retired, Adhesives Industry Sales Manager

"I am thrilled with this book and the simplicity and practicality of its approach.
I especially appreciated the stories and highlights as well as the nuts and bolts to build RDS at our company. I have made it required reading for our business development and leadership teams! We will be implementing this approach in our next monthly meeting."

Kathy Carrier, President and CEO, Brilliant and Keepsake Threads

"Resource-Driven Selling is the most logical argument and conclusion as to why sales people in today's world struggle to drive growth within an organization. This is a MUST read for everyone, including Accountants, Engineers, Shipping Clerks and Customer Service organizations. The anecdotal stories made me laugh and the outlined Core Elements gave me the confidence that as a team, we can change our sales approach and how we retain customers."

Kevin Davis, VP Strategy and Business Development, Amedica Corporation

Selling Without Salespeople

The Death of the "Old-Style" Salesman

Selling Without Salespeople

The Death of the "Old-Style" Salesman

Timothy J. Morrison and Christopher J. Morrison

THE GEODE GROUP

First Edition

ISBN 13: 978-0-615-49472-2
ISBN 10: 0-615-49472-2

Library of Congress Control Number: 2011930932

Contents

Acknowledgements

First and foremost, Chris and I dedicate this book to our families. They provided invaluable patience and support during the financially challenging years as we developed our Resource Driven Selling (RDS) approach and business. We also acknowledge that without the contribution of content and editing by Julianne Morrison and Kyle Morrison, this book in its current state would have not been possible.

We would like to thank:

-The companies who employed our methodology and the many Geode Group coaches and associates, who learned with us and stood by us as our approach evolved.

-The brave souls who took the time and effort to preview and provide feedback on our first publishing endeavor.

-The several truly courageous executives who put their careers on the line by endorsing our concepts even though doing so was often a direct affront to their companies. They could have responded to superiors with malicious obedience, watching ill-conceived strategies fail, but instead they generally risked their reputations by adopting our approach. Their inherent belief that employees attract and retain customers provided us with the canvas to create our life's dream and for that we are very grateful.

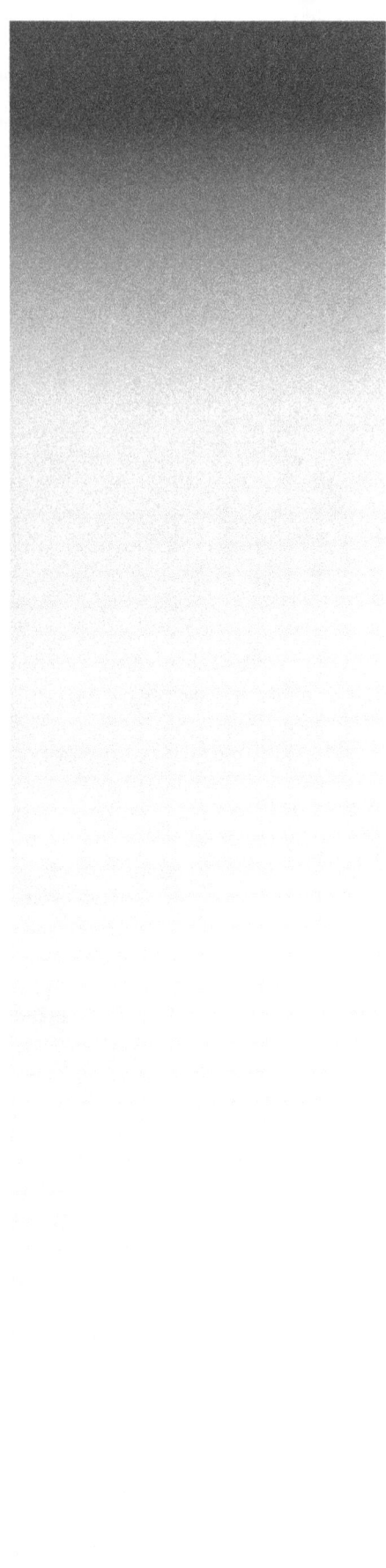

Authors' Notes

Selling Without Salespeople is not a step-by-step, how-to manual or a sales guide for dummies. It does however, explain both the steps to take and to avoid when networking, selling and servicing customers and chronicles how to affect significant change when individuals and companies approach buyers. Although we detail why and how to change outdated approaches to grow and retain customers, we don't do so by moving cheese or conveying topics involving rodents, aquatic life or other nonsensical characters. Several examples based on true stories are used to illustrate aspects of Resource-Driven Selling (RDS), a counter-intuitive approach to selling in today's marketplace. Because *Selling Without Salespeople* is written for multi-departmental resources, and not just salespeople, each chapter will cover the highlights, Epiphanies and Core Elements in a practical and logical format. Because RDS tools are unique to each application or company, they are not included in the book. However, if you require additional detail or would like to customize your own tools, please contact us at info@geodegroup.com and we will provide complementary templates and suggestions.

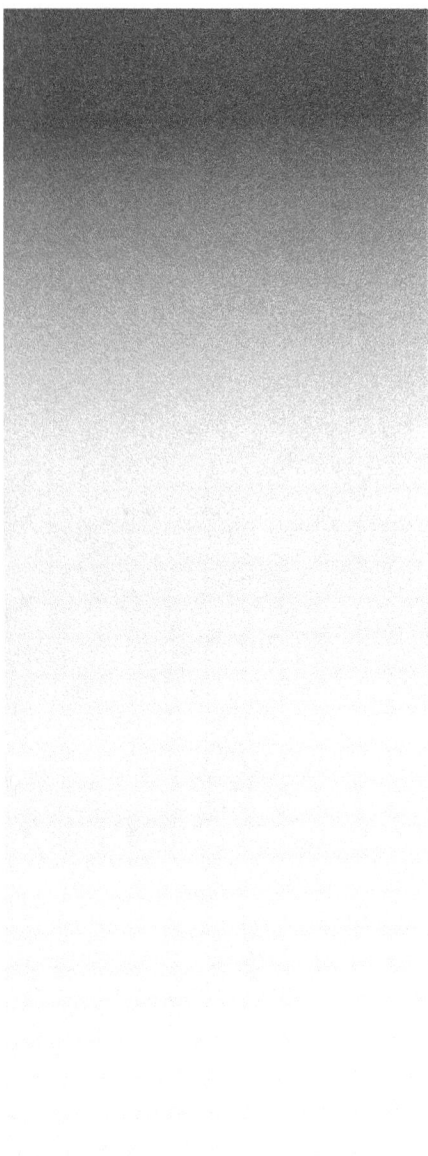

Introduction

Do people buy big-ticket items like flat screen TV's, cars, houses and vacations the way they did 15 years ago? Do they walk into a store or showroom and allow the salesperson to educate and sell them? Do they believe that all salespeople sincerely and objectively educate them on all the features, drawbacks and values of the best product or service available that will suit their needs? Are most consumers more comfortable turning to the Internet to research and review the ratings and ravings of others who already made a similar purchase, or do they prefer to be sold and told what they need by a sales "expert?" To what extent has the reliance on salespeople changed since the introduction of the Internet?

The Internet has changed our culture and continues to modify the way we approach everyday tasks. American business hasn't faced a shift this dramatic since the automotive industry put the buggy whip trade out of business practically overnight. Modern companies in all fields, namely newspapers, banks, book publishers, the music industry, libraries and real estate companies, have been forced to adapt and reinvent themselves by providing online access in order to avoid the fate of the buggy whip companies.

The Internet has changed the manufacturer-driven local and regional marketplaces forcing them to evolve into dynamic consumer-driven, internationally-linked economies lead by consumers. Easy access to product and service options and information has caused this major shift in power. The buying and selling relationship has been impacted even more than any one business, as many sales organizations and salespeople still do not understand why their style, approach and past experiences are ineffective in present day interactions.

The Information Age has dealt a severe blow to the nature of traditional negotiating, forever changing the relationship between sellers and buyers. Information and options equate to power, and this power has clearly shifted from the seller to the buyer. Unlike the last century when salespeople provided brochures, data and a reason to buy, consumers today prefer to research their options and therefore have little need for a salesperson other than to process the purchase agreement. This has made the old-style salesperson practically obsolete and their sales pitches demeaning and often insulting. Thankfully, many of the fast-talking, pushy used car salesmen-types of the 1960's and 1970's have retired. Unfortunately, some old-style salespeople still remain sadly unaware they are being eliminated in cyberspace before their product is even considered as an option by the buyer. Because of the vast amount of information available, many options are eliminated before a salesperson is even contacted.

Please note that although the subtitle of this book

is *The Death of the Old-Style Salesman*, we are not saying *all* salespeople are ineffective or obsolete. In fact, many modern day salespeople tend to have greater ease adapting to and participating in RDS. Some of these individuals, although initially skeptical of RDS, have provided tremendous value to the resource teams and customers, and the results are evident. Salespeople open to contributing and willing to collaborate have become staunch supporters of this approach.

The buying vs. selling shift is not limited to the consumer segment of the market. As consumers, we instinctively take our assumptions and experiences to the workplace. At work, many feel that research and options are just as abundant and in the control of the buyer as they are in personal buying decisions. The buying process itself is no longer as simple as it was ten or fifteen years ago. Many purchasing groups now share the steps of a complex decision-making procurement process with virtually everyone involved in touching the product or service. It seems that today nearly everyone has a voice in approving or blacklisting the options. When purchasing decisions are made by process of elimination and are combined with discussions and/or decisions that take place prior to meeting with a salesperson, the traditional sales process is less effective. A supplier may never know they have been evaluated and disqualified before they even have a chance to speak!

The
Foundation
of RDS

Chapter 1   Unintended Brilliance

Selling Without Salespeople was written to assist organizations and individuals struggling to maintain and grow customer revenue. Many organizations still have an allegiance to communicating with customers within the confines of their traditional organizational structure and therefore fail to utilize the collective expertise necessary to meet a customer's needs. Buying is no longer about being sold. There is an alternative, easy to learn and vastly different way to go about increasing sales revenue.

Most salespeople have confidence, but little depth in understanding the complexities of their own products and services. Many technical resources have that depth, but little confidence in their ability to effectively communicate directly with customers. Today, to meet the buyer's needs, both depth and confidence are essential for success. If you need a compelling reason to alter or change the way you communicate with customers, honestly and objectively look at your own organization. If sales is a silo separate from finance, customer service, technical support, claims and delivery, then perhaps you have found your compelling reason. Resource-Driven Selling (RDS) harnesses multi-departmental depth, providing a balanced resource team with the confidence necessary to grow and retain revenue by assisting buyers to buy. The assumption that the greater the sales experience, the higher the likelihood of success, will be shattered as RDS proves that notion obsolete.

"Buying is no longer about being sold."

I always thought that great inventors were brilliant visionaries who simply sat down and drafted innovative concepts. These innovators introduced something revolutionary while rendering something else obsolete, such as Edison's electric light replacing the candle. When I became part of originating a new way to sell, I didn't feel like a brilliant visionary, nor did I set out to render anything out of date. I wasn't even sure that what we were doing was going to work, let alone be better than the status quo. I've never been known for being a virtuoso or futurist. In fact, in the eighth grade, I think I was silently voted the least likely to succeed. A similar vote may have also have taken place in high school and college. Yet, with an ember of indignant desperation, my partner and I have sparked the creation of a way to increase sales revenue and customer satisfaction, while significantly reducing costs, shortening the sales cycle and virtually eliminating the need for old-style salespeople.

With the creation of RDS, we had shaped a new paradigm, innovative and perhaps so different from the accepted norm that it may have actually preceded the market need. Until a cataclysmic event triggered an anxious market and a once in a lifetime opportunity, there was no appreciable demand for RDS. Our triggering event came compliments of the market crash of September 2008, and the depression-like market contraction that followed.

This unfortunate series of events provided us with an opportunity to prove that non-salespeople can be better at growing and retaining customers than old-style salespeople.

Whether used as a stand-alone process or an overlay to an existing sales process, RDS has proven to be an effective method of growing and retaining customers. When old-style salespeople balked at RDS, we knew we were on to something! What's more, the operations and finance resources found the methodology easy to follow and execute while management applauded the resources for the quick results and cost savings.

When old-style salespeople balked at RDS, we knew we were on to something!

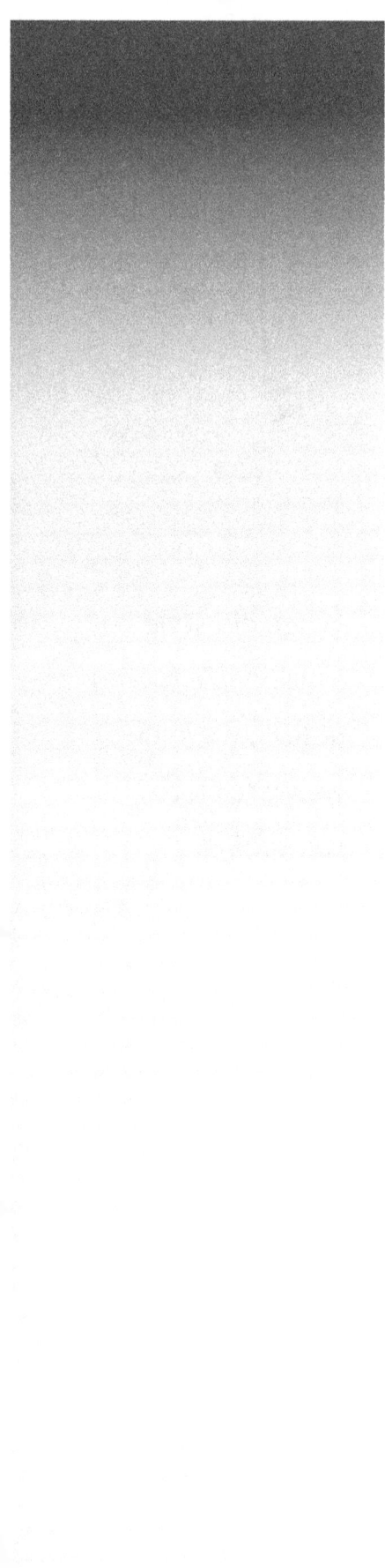

Chapter 2   Roots of the Revolution

CHAPTER SNAPSHOT

• Exploring a better way to approach revenue generation and retention, and getting others to adopt it

• Understanding the benefit of having non-sales, technically proficient resources take the lead

The greatest successes are often times the result of failures, and our company is no exception. Our success was partly the result of a bet made between a CEO and his second in command, that we would fail in our endeavors to help their highly technical, non-sales resources generate revenue. This chapter summarizes how we grew our company with failure-inspired innovation based on the belief that selling has been replaced by buying. Our approach to securing and keeping customers exposes *The 7 Deadly Sales Traps*, the current habits salespeople should avoid at all costs when communicating with prospective and current customers. We will also introduce the foundation of the RDS approach, utilizing non-sales subject matter experts to communicate directly with customers, as they are often better positioned to generate new customer growth and satisfy current customers. When the fear of failure is removed, non-sales resources can be much more effective than some seasoned salespeople who out of habit, continue to sell, tell and push.

> " *When the fear of failure is removed, non-sales resources can be much more effective than some seasoned salespeople who out of habit, continue to sell, tell and push.* "

Many are too young to know or care about the legacy of William Edwards Deming, who is best known for creating Statistical Process Control (SPC), a production improvement technique, in the 1940's. Much like the market crash of 2008 that was the triggering event for RDS, post World War II was Deming's triggering event that provided a decimated Japan with his counter-intuitive approach to manufacturing. Unfortunately, for decades US manufacturers had an "if it ain't broke, don't fix it" complacency and therefore didn't see a need to change until the late 1980's and early 1990's, when it was almost too late. He is pertinent to our story because, like us, he created something that would change the way business was approached, but couldn't get others to try it.

Most people today view Honda and Sony as brands synonymous with quality and value. Much of that credit goes to Deming, as his process shifted Japan's reputation from one of producing cheap junk to delivering consistently innovative, high-quality products, transforming Japan into an economic powerhouse. I vividly recall being required to study SPC in the mid 1980's, when I was a young salesman for Bethlehem Steel. Low cost, high quality steel from Japan nearly put the entire U.S. domestic steel industry out of business. Most of us thought SPC was the latest approach to improving quality, lowering costs and enabling us to compete with the world class Japanese. We were wrong. In reality, we were playing catch up on a process created in the United States in the 1940's but largely ignored until the 1980's when it was almost too late. The Japanese innovation, growth and profitability looked like a lot more fun than the decade of red ink and salary and job cuts the domestic steel industry endured. Although still involving immense change, being the first to innovate usually results in proactive, not reactive, process and attitude changes. Japanese innovation lead to cost advantages and global market share growth as well as soaring profitability and employment security, but for the domestic steel industry, playing catch up meant just the opposite. I left the steel industry to try my hand at processing and distribution, and ultimately high tech telecom, but all seemed to be plagued with similar catch up afflictions.

In 2003, after 24 years in various front line and management positions, I decided to leave the bombardment of catchy buzzwords, acronyms and frequently re-spun narratives of corporate America and start over. I had worked in large and small, public and private, manufacturing and service, high and low tech companies. Although each was different in what they produced and sold, all were approaching their employees and customers basically the same way others had for over 30 years. Even though I grew up in sales, I knew there had to be a better way to increase revenue and retain customers. I also knew that if a better

Although still involving immense change, being the first to innovate usually results in proactive, not reactive, process and attitude changes.

CORE ELEMENT 1

Embrace Negative Planning for Positive Results

Negative Planning exposes and minimizes the risk for failure by concentrating on what can go wrong before anything actually goes wrong. Anticipating the worst from a buyer's viewpoint (what they might say or do) can help prepare a resource team with valuable, proactive, problem solving solutions. Traditional sales approaches focus on the positive outcomes a salesperson may hope will happen. A can-do sales attitude can be another term for happy ears. Resources with happy ears successfully sell themselves but often fail to understand what it takes to satisfy a customer.

way was ever devised, the Kool-Aid drinking, old-school traditionalists would dismiss it immediately as a threat to how they sold. I needed a fresh approach from experienced individuals who were capable of identifying what needs to change by understanding what does not work as well as works. I thought that entrepreneurs with corporate experience would know exactly what to do, what to avoid and how to create an entirely new approach. The problem is that corporate America, although known for entrepreneurs and seasoned executives, appears to lack the combination of both virtues in one individual. Therefore, I decided it would be easier to create the type of innovators I needed than attempt to find them.

I solicited the help of my brother Chris, a seasoned sales professional from the service sector. I didn't ask Chris to help because he was known as a risk taking genius, but because I knew that together, we could try and fail and try again until we could succeed at creating a better way to sell. Despite coming from completely different backgrounds, Chris had similar concerns with the selling and buying trends I saw emerging. Chris sold financial and high tech services for over twenty years, providing a much needed viewpoint. I trusted him and knew he would challenge me, question me and tell me when I was full of crap - something he relished.

Chris and I were considered "experienced," but neither one of us had been labeled an entrepreneur, at least not since we cut grass and painted houses in high school and college. However, we were ready to explore the possibility of trying something completely different, since we knew that the selling we grew up with had changed. Few businesses, if any, recognized the paradigm shift we clearly saw, and none appeared poised to adapt to the change. We felt the market void would eventually present an opportunity, so we decided to create a completely different approach to growing and retaining customers. We started by mapping the flow of what failed and why in our vastly different careers. Mapping those failures led us to the first of 10 Core Elements, Embrace Negative Planning for Positive Results. Negative Planning is nothing more than putting oneself in the customer's shoes and then second-guessing and shooting holes in one's own approach. It is anticipating issues and concerns that the customer may have at any time during the buying process. A team that plans for the worst from the customer's viewpoint is generally better prepared to realize root customer needs and concerns and therefore provide valuable suggestions and solutions that will build mutual trust and respect between the buyer and seller.

Although Chris sold accounting services and technology solutions to the banking industry, he had no formal

> *Negative Planning is nothing more than putting oneself in the customer's shoes and then second-guessing and shooting holes in one's own approach.*

finance education or training. I sold steel products and steel processing and distribution services, but was not an engineer or metallurgist. We both worked for the same company selling teleconferencing products and services before launching our consulting business and neither one of us had electronic or engineering education. Aside from the differences in our education and work experience, we knew we could work together. We also shared an appreciation for the times we failed as salespeople, since most of our collective failures were linked to attempts to sell without involving a technically proficient resource, a foundational and very essential element of RDS.

The Negative Planning for Positive Results concept evolved into a fundamental yet comprehensive communication approach. RDS is the final product of our Negative Planning brainstorming sessions because it is rooted in Negative Planning, but it is much more than just planning and Negative Planning. RDS utilizes a blend of non-sales resources throughout an organization and enhances, or even replaces old-style salespeople. The probability of earning new customers and retaining current ones is amplified with this approach. Cross-functional resources plan for and pursue only prospective buyers who clearly demonstrate a considerable possibility of becoming a customer. The resources can be mostly non-sales, subject matter experts from every discipline of the organization.

The early drafts of RDS made one thing abundantly clear: this approach needed to be based on our own experiences and our collective success was more the result of avoiding failure than targeting success. Therefore, we based much of our initial approach on an atypical philosophy rooted in the belief that fear of failure causes people involved in selling to act differently, not always appropriately. However, when that fear of failure is minimized or removed, individuals involved with the customer tend to approach selling with genuine empathy and therefore can be more willing to make "selling" or directly communicating with prospects and customers a common practice in their day-to-day duties.

The RDS approach evolved much the way I learned to swim. My first swim lesson was not intended to teach me great Olympic swim techniques; I swam simply to keep from drowning. With that in mind, we set out to design a methodology that relies on a common sense, no BS approach to basic and direct communication that keeps the participant from failing, being rejected or being told "no." We decided to minimize the likelihood of failure in order to increase the likelihood of success and in turn, build confidence and courage, two essential attributes for communicating with customers. The basic blocking and tackling techniques at the root are nothing more than a simple, honest and empathetic approach to first learning what, if anything, the buyer needs and then honestly

RDS eliminates aggressive old-style selling, making presentations and issuing pricing from a sales process. It can remove selling from selling!

EPIPHANY

1

Remove the 7 Deadly Sales Traps

Eliminating the following seven bad habits reduces the risk of failure and increases the likelihood of success.

1. Relationship selling.

2. Selling, presenting and promoting one's product or service.

3. Pitching one's value or solution when the customer voices a need.

4. Approaching from a perspective other than the customer's.

5. Drawing conclusions based on gut instinct or what one thinks, not what one knows to be a fact as specifically related by the customer.

6. Closing, telling and/or issuing price proposals.

7. Confident, experienced salespeople "Winging it" rather than planning and Negative Planning from the customer's viewpoint.

assessing if there is a fit between the buyer's need and the seller's sustained deliverable. This can be very difficult for some old-style salespeople who will do what they can to sell their product or service, regardless of whether there is a direct and exact need by the customer.

We assembled several hundred typical scenarios in an effort to expose even the slightest possibility of losing a customer or being rejected by a prospective customer. This proved to be a daunting task, as it was impossible to anticipate everything that might go wrong in every possible scenario, in every kind of business. We conducted our own Negative Planning for Positive Results. This excruciatingly self-reflective, devil's advocate approach to what went wrong in a variety of painful experiences was essential in the evolution of RDS.

Listing the ideal win/win for each scenario, we drilled down to better understand what it would take to achieve a desired outcome. After shooting holes in a host of scenarios, it became clear that whether the products and/or services are expensive or inexpensive, durable or non-durable, large or small, the approach to selling the products and services may differ, however, the actions and behaviors that threaten or actually result in failure, are nearly identical.

As we studied this pattern, we had our first Epiphany, that regardless of the product or service, the likelihood of failing to earn a new customer, or keep an existing one was usually related to several selling faux pas. Coincidentally, many of these were the same practices generally accepted by old school salespeople. We categorized them as *The 7 Deadly Sales Traps*, as illustrated in the left margin. Ironically, these killers of customer trust and relationships can be similar to approaches deployed by old-style salespeople and in some instances are still taught to sales teams today.

We concluded that since the root cause for the majority of sales failures could be identified, isolated, minimized or eliminated, we needed to prevent the resource team from falling into these deadly traps. As we designed RDS, we removed the traps and emphasized new Core Elements that would steer our clients away from following commonly practiced, but often flawed approaches. We then fine-tuned our approach to work with a variety of organizations in virtually any industry.

Reviewing *The 7 Deadly Sales Traps* shows exactly why RDS can be somewhat controversial. RDS eliminates aggressive old-style selling, making presentations and issuing pricing from a sales process. It can remove selling from selling! It focuses on the how the buyer buys, not the how the seller sells. It puts relationship selling in a different light, focusing on relationships forged from trust-based and customer-centric interactions. RDS advocates the Negative Planning of what could go wrong rather than perpetuating

> " We then fine-tuned our approach to work with a variety of organizations in virtually any industry. "

an obligatory positive can-do "selling" attitude. Most old school salespeople will tell you that selling is about relationship and positive attitude, so to them this approach can be unconventional and even uncomfortable. In fact, RDS is counter to what many salespeople and organizations have been doing for decades. Therefore, in order to test our counter-intuitive approach, we needed to find immensely unsuccessful organizations. Finding them was not difficult; convincing them to let us help proved to be the hurdle.

We targeted results-challenged organizations because in theory, they would be more open to change what was causing them to fall short of their goals. Our assumption was that organizations who were sick and afraid of dying will risk trying an experimental cure if it means getting well again. We viewed ourselves as revenue doctors, ready to help those who knew they needed help. We were wrong, because companies in desperate need of revenue couldn't afford to hire us. Those who could, didn't have the intestinal fortitude to implement a different approach because they were just one mistake away from bankruptcy. So we went back and fine-tuned our RDS approach, hoping that someone other than us would see its value.

Having technically proficient non-sales, subject matter experts completely involved and often taking the lead in the sales effort, although counter to most sales approaches, quickly became the cornerstone of RDS. In other words, RDS was specifically designed to be executed by a blended team of resources. Our intention was to get the non-sales resources to feel comfortable assisting salespeople in retaining and generating customers, encouraging them to get involved and provide support and credibility for the sales team. Most salespeople will admit that those who create the product or service can be very helpful in representing and promoting it; but that is generally where the credit from some salespeople ends. Most salespeople use operations, technical support and internal service providers for sales support, but very often the salesperson still takes credit for the sale, the customer relationship and of course the revenue generated. This approach generally does not foster a great deal of trust, respect, or solidarity with the rest of the team, or in many cases the customer. It also is not effective because a salesperson that tells, sells, distributes brochures and promotes features or price can strip away the credibility earned by non-sales, subject matter resources.

Some non-salespeople are better equipped to genuinely approach customers with empathy, quickly generating the trust and credibility necessary to maintain and grow relationships. Unfortunately, our first major challenge was most of the technically savvy subject matter experts were incredibly uncomfortable with the idea of making a sales call and said they would rather lose a limb than be

> *Some non-salespeople are better equipped to genuinely approach customers with empathy, quickly generating the trust and credibility necessary to maintain and grow relationships.*

CORE
ELEMENT
2

Better Positioning Non-Sales Resources to Satisfy Customer Needs

Selling has been replaced by buying because service and sincerity build trust and trust is essential in a buyer/seller relationship. Non-sales resources can be more credible and effective than old-style salespeople who continue to sell, tell and push products and services. Those who make and deliver the product and/ or service to the customer can earn more credibility and trust because they view themselves as problem solvers who create and deliver, not salespeople who make promises.

considered part of the sales team. This phenomenon of dismissing old-style salespeople as extraneous was not just limited to the non-salespeople in the companies we encountered. We found that it was also widely shared by buyers, senior level decision makers and people in general and therefore resource team selling became the cornerstone and second Core Element of RDS.

For us, denouncing "sales" was the equivalent of changing the very fiber of our being and starting over again. Although we were both the product of countless sales training programs and had read most of the trendy motivational books over the years, it wasn't until we truly looked at selling from the customer's viewpoint that we realized we had to change nearly everything in our approach to selling. We had lived and breathed *The 7 Deadly Sales Traps* and struggled to remove them from our ingrained habits. If we didn't turn our own preconceived, experienced-based assumptions upside down and inside out, we'd end up wasting RDS and time on just stubborn, old school salespeople. Experience demonstrates that most salespeople get momentarily fired up, but ultimately revert back to old and comfortable habits, even when given a new approach and opportunity to change. Since RDS advocates change we decided to concentrate on people and organizations eager for permanent change. To increase the odds of success, we embarked on a revenue growth and retention approach

that would signal the death of the old-style salesman and introduce a true team selling enhancement to any sales process.

We didn't get there overnight. In fact, RDS was initially nothing more than Sales 101 for non-salespeople. But what we encountered was an increasing trend of people who historically had little to do with selling, but needed to learn sales techniques because of changes in their responsibilities. Our target became individuals with new business development and revenue accountability as part of their responsibilities. We expanded our focus to include struggling and inexperienced salespeople as well as highly skilled subject matter experts. Both groups needed help learning how to better communicate internally and with customers. Some engineers, pharmacists, and state economic development people welcomed the help. Old school sales and customer service people, although reluctant to change their self-imagined stellar sales styles, were included, if for no other reason than to prevent them from sabotaging our efforts to include the non-sales resources. We found old-style salespeople to be the biggest obstacle in generating sales revenue when involving subject matter experts. Some very effective salespeople embraced RDS and appreciated the help. However, old-style salespeople routinely insist on holding their coveted customer relationships hostage from their employers and peers, which

We encountered an increasing trend of people who historically had little to do with selling, but needed to learn sales techniques.

is counter to RDS and the good of the corporation and the customer.

Old school salespeople are bred to dominate, control and covet customer relationships, sales credit, praise and money, because salespeople in general experience more rejection and failure than most in a typical organization. A win that is preceded by ten humiliating losses is cherished and celebrated with boastful glee by most sales professionals. It makes sense; Salespeople commemorate their own success because their value and job security is based on what they win, so self-proclaimed credit is a matter of survival.

As a salesperson I was no different. In 1990, as a young sales manager for Bethlehem Steel, I recall our CEO speaking to a room full of middle and senior level executives from every discipline in the corporation. He said that there were really only two groups in the company, those who made the steel and those who sold it. He went on to say that everyone else in the company was there to support operations and sales. At the time, I was thrilled to confirm what I always knew: salespeople were on top of the food chain. Unfortunately, like most salespeople at the time, I actually believed it, which fed my over-inflated ego and sales arrogance.

It took thirteen years and that little thing called the Internet to help me realize that selling and telling customers why they need to buy is no longer necessary. If Bethlehem Steel had not gone out of business, I would love to tell their former CEO that the focus should be on only one group in any growing organization. It's not management, sales, marketing, operations, or finance; it is the combined group of cross-functional resources, creating and providing a product or service to the customer. These subject matter experts can be coached to provide credible information to customers who use or need what the company provides. I recently heard someone say, "Service is the new sales." My reaction was "Oh great, another cheesy catchphrase," but then after reflecting on the statement, I had to agree that in many cases, those who service have in fact replaced those who sell. The root of the problem with the non-sales service group isn't a lack of skills, experience or ability in sales and service; they lack the time necessary to service customers and foster relationships because they have other full time jobs. Until RDS, dealing with customers was neither a priority nor what non-sales resources considered their core competency.

The start of our revenue generating consulting business in 2003 was truly a blessing, or as we say now, dumb luck. We attribute much of our humble beginnings and initial success to simply helping dysfunctional organizations take advantage of the strength of a very bullish market. Unless our clients blatantly shot themselves in the foot, (which

> *Until RDS, dealing with customers was neither a priority nor what non-sales resources considered their core competency.*

> *We catagorized some extremely conservative targets as low probability because of their resistance to change their affiliation with old-school industries.*

happened more often than not) most experienced growth, despite their ineptness in business development and the evolving RDS approach. Our early clients appeared to have good products and services but lacked focus and a simple strategy to deliver them. They were, however, very skilled at shooting themselves in the foot, so our guidance, although unpolished, proved to be immensely successful.

By spring 2007 we had exhausted our supply of struggling, dysfunctional clients who had enough of a budget to pay for our services. We categorized some extremely conservative targets as a low probability because of their resistance to change or their affiliation with old school industries. For instance, most accountants proved to be too conservative to take a risk. Most engineers were initially interested, but required way too much proof. Many lawyers appeared to us to be nothing more than accountants with arrogance and attitude, which prevented them from admitting weakness or asking for help. Our small, privately held clients lacked the means to execute our rapidly emerging RDS. Our Negative Planning provided a very painful yet eye-opening reality; we had unintentionally disqualified nearly all of our potential customers. We therefore decided to subscribe to that old adage from many a labor union, "Give me dignity or give me death." We chose death and decided to blow up our company if we couldn't find someone to recognize they needed a better

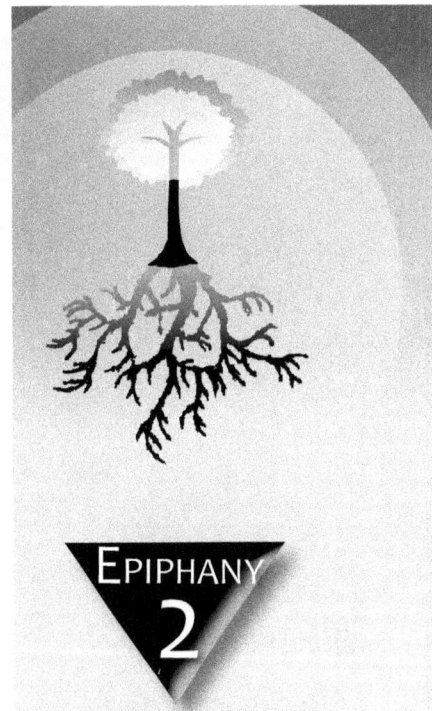

Redirect Fear to Inspire Risk-Taking and Courage

When there is a feeling that there is nothing left to lose, combining courage with basic survival instincts is intuitively more effective than conservative or politically correct actions and reactions.

way to sell. We jokingly called this self-destruct approach "Kobayashi Maru," the scenario made famous in Star Trek. Like the crew of the Starship Enterprise, we found ourselves in a no-win situation. We had a unique method, but no significant customers. Without customers, we lacked the income we needed to prevent us from having to put our tails between our legs and crawl back to corporate America to sales positions that promoted an outdated and inefficient sales process we no longer could tolerate. Like Star Trek's Captain Kirk (the only federation cadet to deceive death by cheating on the Kobayashi Maru test), we needed a bold plan to cheat the death of our dream. We decided to test our innovative approach on someone who needed it. The problem was finding a customer who needed it.

With nothing to lose, we targeted struggling multi-billion dollar corporations who were willing to supplement their current sales process structure. They also had to be willing to do so in a matter of weeks – the time frame in which we needed to land something before closing our doors. Obviously, the odds were stacked against us. In fact, our second Epiphany was the direct result of the fact that there was no possible way to win. Knowing we could not win and failure was inevitable, our fear of failure disappeared, creating the courage and attitude it took to say and do things we never would have in the past. Similar to how an animal backed into a corner behaves differently with

> *Our theory was if RDS succeeded in generating sales, logically, in reverse it should help procurement people to procure more effectively.*

no possible way to win and countless ways to lose, we decided to behave like we didn't have a care in the world, as though clients were banging down our door. Our desperate arrogance lead us to a friend of Chris' from the consumer goods industry who was well connected with high-level buyers in a $7 billion grocery distribution company. Within two weeks, we were in front of the entire procurement group's management team. Our networking worked like a charm, but we had failed to consider that in addition to being a two-person company attempting to diagnose and cure the ills of a $7 billion corporation, neither of us had any consumer goods retail experience. If that was not bad enough, we were about to pitch a sales revenue generating approach to a purchasing team! Other than that, our plan was spot on.

With two weeks to prepare, we needed a crash course in grocery industry acumen and issues and worked on feverishly turning our sales growth and retention methodology inside out. Our theory was if RDS succeeded in generating sales, logically, in reverse it should help procurement people to procure more effectively. I remember thinking we had finally crossed the line. Chris and I were two former salespeople, who designed an approach that could eliminate the need for old-style salespeople. We were helping a purchasing group gain even more power and control over their vendors by manipulating and out negotiating vendor teams. Although we felt a little like Benedict Arnold, we knew we had very limited time to cheat death and find some way to keep our dream alive. We had nothing to lose!

To our amazement, our discussion with the procurement team was very well received. In fact, we had a series of follow up discussions and genuine interest before we actually deemed them a very low likelihood prospect. Within days of expressing their interest in our reverse RDS, we realized that our $7 billion lifeline was out of control and therefore out of our reach. Why? Because they lacked the ability to handle the immense volume of voice mails, emails and meeting requests that plagued their day. Without basic, simple communication and follow up, our resource driven buying pilot would fall on deaf ears (or no ears in this case) and waste our clients money and our time, rendering our assistance unnecessary to them and frustrating to us. We had to decide whether to chance out-waiting this giant conglomerate of miscommunication or quickly move on to opportunities with a higher likelihood. Despite their sincere interest, our calls and emails were not returned, so we shifted our focus to Plan B. This lesson is one we still emphasize today - spend time where results are possible. Don't labor where you want to succeed, focus where you can succeed.

Don't labor where you want to succeed, focus on where you can succeed.

We learned several things from the dead end adventure with the procurement group. First, by turning RDS inside out in order to benefit buyers, we reaffirmed what buyers expected from sellers and now we knew from being in the buyers shoes that RDS worked. We knew the need for a more current approach to selling was as important to multi-billion dollar organizations as it was in the much smaller clients we had serviced. Our crash course in the grocery procurement business also taught us how crucial it is not just to understand the buyer's perspective, but to plan every aspect of the buyer/seller relationship solely with the buyer's needs, concerns and expectations top of mind.

If our dream to keep our company alive was to be successful, we had to quickly move on and find other options. Chris found an opportunity for us as facilitators for a Certified Public Accountants association semi-annual meeting. I was impressed that he secured something so quickly. Then I learned that we were not being paid. Like Watergate's Deep Throat, my initial suggestion to Chris was to follow the money. Then I realized at least we had exposure to potential clients so we'd better get to work and develop something that would catch and keep the attention of a room full of accountants. Other than lighting the room on fire and setting off the sprinkler system, we were at a loss for something that would excite a room with 50 accountants. With a little Negative Planning we decided to expose one of the accounting trades' greatest nightmares. We entitled our session "Your Financial Forecast is Only as Good as Your Worst Salesman." Our idea was to get the attention of CFO's who surely would see the value we could provide. The session was a huge success and for what it was worth, we scored the highest grade of all the days' sessions. Unfortunately, quantifiable leads were non-existent as was our income. The same group asked us to write an article for their quarterly CPA magazine. Again, in an effort to gain some visibility, we agreed to do so, albeit pro-bono because accountants are somewhat frugal. Drawing on the communication disaster we had just experienced with our short-lived grocery procurement target, our article was cleverly titled *"Who Has Time for Anything But Email?"* which dealt with the daily onslaught of high tech communication vehicles overwhelming most individuals and organizations. It had nothing to do with our core competency, but, as Chris kept telling me, it was exposure. Credit was given to just one author, so it was exciting, at least for me, to be "published." Chris won't admit it, but he never really got over it, so to this day I tell everyone that although he helped me write the article, his job was to do what he did best - to capitalize on my notoriety. That too failed, so I guess we were even. I began to wonder if Edison had to struggle this long to dethrone a lousy candle.

Just as we were about to breathe our last breath, we got

> *I began to wonder if Edison had to struggle this long to dethrone a lousy candle.*

> *We responded in a way that would significantly increase the odds of getting an audience with the actual decision makers.*

a call from a network contact who asked us to provide a quote for developing and delivering a survey to employees and customers of another multi-billion dollar corporation. The opportunity involved helping this corporation roll out both internal and external messages based on their perceived image. Historically, we had refused to respond to formal Request for Proposal (RFP), so our first instinct was to walk away. But we thought of our soon-to-be-starving kids and decided to respond to the RFP. However, our response was somewhat unconventional by design. We responded in a way that would significantly increase the odds of getting an audience with the actual decision makers, so that we could question their need for RDS. We were still trying to cheat death, so anything that could provide a venue to test our concept was worth a shot.

We broke all the rules we had established and fired off a price quote with a letter detailing the scope of our undertaking. We outsourced data collection, minus the management interviews, because the scope of the job was out of our comfort zone, but it paid! Our proposal gave the customer exactly what they requested, but we created a clear point of confusion and a great deal of intrigue so that those screening the proposals would be forced to realize they couldn't compare apples to apples with our bid. We knew no one else could possibly have provided more than what was required, so we figured we'd either be called in by the actual decision makers for a follow up discussion, or be immediately dismissed as insane by the bid screener.

The differentiator in the bid was a free assessment to "pilot" RDS within their operation as we conducted the messaging survey. This corporation was actually several hundred independent acquisitions in need of a united, internal and external message as indicated by their RFP. Brainstorming, combined with the research, allowed us to connect a few dots. We made the assumption that their declining sales were connected to their failure to position their highly complex solutions in a way that satisfied their fairly low-tech, unsophisticated customers. Our gamble to deviate from the standard RFP format, combined with our research, brainstorming and Negative Planning paid off. At last, a door was opened and RDS could be covertly piloted! But even our superior Negative Planning skills would be tested and stretched in the next series of events.

We tested and slowly implemented our concepts with pharmacists, nurses, billing coordinators and medical technicians over the next year and a half, but only after being set up for what felt like a scene right out of Eddie Murphy's *Trading Places* movie. Our "pilot" appeared to be a secret bet between the skeptical CEO of the pharmacy service company and a fellow executive over whether we, or anyone else, could teach pharmacists to sell. The

CEO stacked the deck by presenting us with a group of pharmacists who apparently couldn't sell if their lives depended on it. Adding insult to injury, in our first internal messaging interview, we asked the Senior VP of Operations what the company's average sales cycle was from prospect to signed contract. On average, it took about eighteen months for the best salespeople, but as Senior VP of Operations and the self-proclaimed best salesperson in the company, he was known to occasionally shorten that cycle to seven months. After learning about their seven to eighteen month sales cycle, we realized we had just been duped by the CEO and had guaranteed that at least one of the introverted pharmacists would take a prospect to a signed contract by the company's annual conference, which was just four weeks away.

Following a quick assessment of the ringers the CEO provided us with, we immediately realized that the pharmacists in our group, although not a finely tuned sales machine, were all genuinely good people who wanted to help grow their business but didn't know how. Unfortunately, we didn't have time to teach them how to do anything other than to quickly disqualify everything that could not close in less than four weeks. We were right back in the no-win scenario. It was either time for another Kobayashi Maru to cheat death or to plan to help our team of subject matter experts to successfully disqualify low probability prospects and reveal the few possibilities having interest. We elected to go with the disqualifying because it was a major component of RDS and after all, we were trying to pilot RDS, not cheat death anymore. However, in a matter of a few days, death appeared to be inevitable once again because we collectively disqualified everything the team brought to us. But we stuck to our plan!

One of the pharmacists involved in the pilot casually mentioned he had a mildly interested prospective customer who was scheduled to come in for a pharmacy tour later that week. After asking a couple dozen questions, it was apparent to us that the pharmacy team knew nothing about this prospective customer and knew even less about how to turn the pharmacy tour into an opportunity. Based on the wisdom gained in this brief discussion, we concluded there was no chance to close this, or any other deal in the three weeks that remained. At this point, we deployed a planning segment of RDS and helped the pharmacy team prepare to host their guests. Our intention was to walk them through the planning process. Interestingly, the low probability of success removed the team's pressure to succeed. Similar to the time we removed our fear of failure with the Kobayashi Maru, our once reluctant and apprehensive resource team was now engaged, motivated and very eager to get involved because they genuinely felt there was no way to win or lose.

Interestingly, the low probability of success removed the team's pressure to succeed.

Step one was to prepare Carl, the Pharmacy Manager, for a call to the VP of the prospective customer. It was imperative to know all of our guests and their common expectations. Carl and the VP agreed to expand the morning visit to include lunch and a reciprocal tour of the VP's facility immediately following the pharmacy tour. A joint agenda was set and we went to work. With a list of attendees, we called in the pharmacy's billing coordinator, nurses, a consultant pharmacist, several customer service representatives, Carl and his Regional Director. Each resource was given a theme, questions to ask and questions to prepare for if asked. Their individual theme was a simple topic or message they were to deliver. For instance, one of the customer service representatives was to point out that he lived within a mile of one of the prospective customer's facilities and drove past another facility every day on his way to and from work. The message was that he was local and could stop by anytime an issue arose.

The seating was arranged to pair our resources with each visiting team member according to job function. Carl's introduction was scripted and rehearsed to ensure that the session came across as a joint approach with participation from both the prospective customer and our resource team. When the morning's pairings were complete, we asked Linda, the billing coordinator, to take on a special function. Linda was asked to take the prospective customer's

Accounts Payable person and CFO to her workstation. Linda's theme was to get her guests to feel comfortable with her, not to sell or promote anything. Linda asked if she could share pictures of her grandchildren with her guests in order to get personally acquainted. Linda's idea was incorporated into her general theme and it was extended to all resources to help showcase the entire pharmacy as warm and personable.

We hastily took casual pictures of all key pharmacy staff members and created a "Personalized Bio Book" that contained each resource's education, work experience, job function and perceived value to the customer, and each of the resource's photos. We created a visual map of our pharmacy locations, the prospective customer's facilities and contact information for our team. Because the pharmacy had a reputation of being the 800-pound, impersonal gorilla in the area, we also noted the residences of the pharmacy's key employees to illustrate how many of the employees lived near their facilities and could physically check in whenever needed.

The tours and lunch went as planned, without a salesperson present. Our blended team of well-prepared management and technical resources felt very comfortable with the task at hand. That comfort led to confidence, as they answered questions with sincere empathy and

> *That comfort led to confidence, as they answered questions with sincere empathy and expertise.*

> *This recognition was particularly beneficial because it built their confidence and encouraged the team to do it all over again.*

expertise. Linda, initially terrified at the team planning sessions, managed to make the accounts payable person and the CFO feel comfortable. In fact, because Linda wasn't focused on "selling," the CFO, who initially resisted changing pharmacy providers trusted Linda enough to consider a change. The proof was quickly revealed the next day when the CFO invited Linda to a detailed follow up meeting. Trust had been established and the follow up calls between resources on both sides became too numerous to count. The customer revealed several concerns with their current pharmacy and actually commented that the bio book and joint meetings made them feel very comfortable knowing they could have the best of both worlds - a high service local team backed by a major corporation.

Chris and I planned to attend the company's annual conference and report our survey findings to over 250 senior managers and reluctantly admit that the RDS pilot produced no revenue results. However, one hour prior to ascending to the stage, Carl told us the facility VP had just signed the contract. As we came to the close of our session, we announced to the CEO and the entire management team that the RDS pilot had generated a $4 million contract. Carl and members of his team were recognized for shattering the company's record of taking a prospect to a signed contract in four weeks. This recognition was particularly beneficial because it built their confidence and encouraged the team to do it all over again.

The CEO, although dozing on and off during our time on stage, woke up long enough to dismiss our success as "luck." However, within a few weeks, our initial luck was enough to get us a second challenge to do it again, which we did, and did again and again until we were asked to roll our RDS approach out throughout the country. We had cash flow, but more importantly, a customer who wanted to use every aspect of RDS.

In the early days it could be argued each of our client's successes came a little from added structure and a lot from the booming marketplace, but in late 2008, everything abruptly changed with the market crash that continued throughout 2009 and 2010. It wasn't until the summer of 2009 that we actually realized that RDS was a lot more than just Sales 101 for dysfunctional organizations and non-salespeople. Despite all our training and sales experience, we had accidently created a simple and effective way for nearly any organization, even in the worst of economic downturns, to consistently increase revenue while drastically reducing costs. We had created Sales 101 without the need for old-style salespeople and their associated cost. It was the perfect storm. In 2009, one of the worst economic downturns in 50 years, while most companies retracted and cut costs, RDS delivered an increase in new customer

sales and provided improved customer retention. RDS had contributed $1.94 billion of new growth and retained revenue for our clients in just 24 months. Achieving these results in a marketplace where most companies were cutting employees and doing everything possible just to survive, proved to our clients that RDS was not only efficient, it was a valuable way to cut costs and expand revenue, feats rarely accomplished in tandem.

Chapter 2 Highlights

1. RDS Core Elements and Epiphanies can be counter-intuitive. Core Elements are generally positive habits and communication approaches; Epiphanies can be negative or bad habits that if not eliminated can prevent the Core Elements from being successfully implemented. Both can provide positive outcomes.
2. The first Core Element, *Embrace Negative Planning for Positive Results,* exposes and minimizes the risk of failure by concentrating on what can go wrong, not just the positive outcome hoped for.
3. The first Epiphany, *The 7 Deadly Sales Traps,* are the negative attributes and actions often touted as the habits old school salespeople practice and strive for.
4. The second Core Element, *Better Positioning Non-Sales Resources to Satisfy Customer Needs,* infers that some non-sales, subject matter experts are better positioned to satisfy customer growth and retention needs. Buying has replaced selling because service and sincerity sell – therefore non-salespeople can be more effective than old school

salespeople who continue to sell, tell and push.

5. Team planning for each aspect of important customer interactions and communication boosts confidence in blended resource teams.

6. The second Epiphany is to *Redirect Fear to Inspire Risk-Taking and Courage*. Similar to an animal backed into a corner with no other option than to fight its way out, the second Epiphany encourages more risk and courage. Failure breeds innovation and innovation breeds success.

7. Well planned meeting agendas and supporting materials provide focus and help to properly establish expectations. Plan and verbalize everything as a team. If it sounds canned or slick to you, it will also sound that way to the customer!

8. RDS can be an effective way to significantly reduce costs, shrink sales cycle time and maximize revenue.

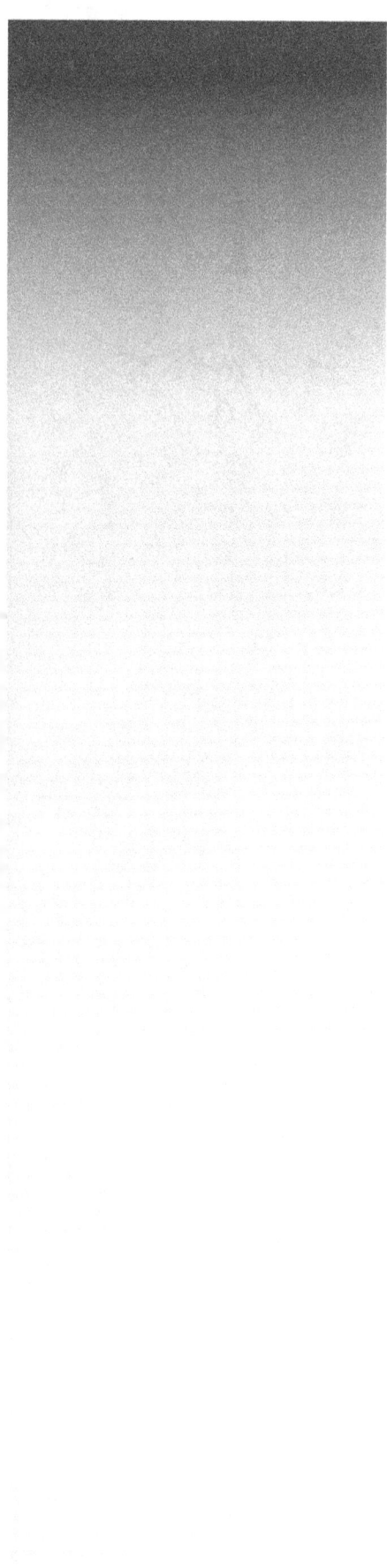

Chapter 3 Assessing & Balancing Resource Strength

CHAPTER SNAPSHOT

• Effectively communicating internally and directly with customers, utilizing well-balanced resource teams; People do business with people, not just one person

• Assessing the entire team's strengths and building a balanced team based on behavioral styles, job responsibilities and expertise

In this chapter we will introduce why resource team involvement, if properly planned can produce faster, more consistent results, demonstrating why RDS can better motivate and satisfy both employees and customers. But none of this can be accomplished until letting go of some well-entrenched assumptions and practices. Therefore, we ask each reader (especially those in management) to consider a counter-intuitive and perhaps uncomfortable approach of trusting non-salespeople with managing customer relationships.

Once tested and fully developed, we knew that RDS was not for the faint of heart. Investing in this counter-intuitive approach, although not necessarily viewed as risky, clearly takes some intestinal fortitude to alter what has always been done. We knew it was a no-brainer for most organizations to want a different way to reduce their cost of sales, shorten the sales cycle and increase new and existing customer revenue. However, we also strongly suspected that many

> " Investing in this counter-intuitive approach, although not necessarily viewed as risky, clearly takes some intestinal fortitude to alter what has always been done. "

> *Their staunch loyalty to their own coveted traditions often prevents them from executing leading edge business development change of any consequence.*

lacked the courage to submit their organizations to such a crucial, albeit necessary transformation, because few have the courage to change what they may not yet see as broken. Although we believed we had a tiger by the tail, we had to become highly selective in qualifying our clients. We wanted to work with those who could succeed because they realized their sales and retention approach needed adjustments. Since most organizations we observed seemed to be selling virtually the same way, we needed to identify only those willing to take a risk and adopt an approach of which few were even aware. Therefore, we initially disqualified highly structured, traditional cultures with decades of sales policies and procedural sacred cows as having very low likelihood of embracing an add-on methodology like RDS. This type of culture would likely resist a Kobayashi Maru that would force them to start over with a new selling philosophy. Also highly conservative executives, companies and industries such as accounting and law firms were again temporarily disqualified, even though they were ideal for the RDS business development application. We learned that these types of individuals and organizations are generally too slow to act in advance of changing market trends. Their staunch loyalty to their own coveted traditions often prevents them from executing leading edge business development change of any consequence.

Although RDS has a lot of moving and integrated

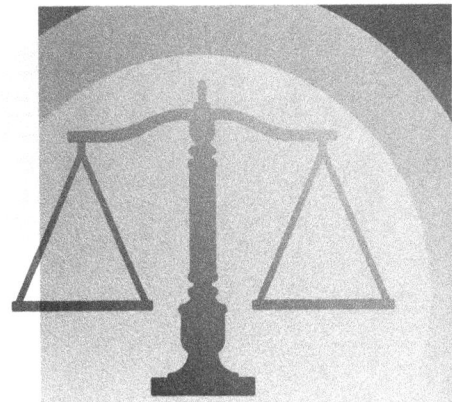

components, it is not complicated. It does however, contain enough structure that if cherry picked, it will not be as effective. Therefore, organizations and/or individuals who wanted to quickly implement specific aspects of RDS, but lacked the commitment to fully engage the entire methodology were also dismissed. As I'm sure you've surmised by now, we successfully disqualified the majority of prospective clients and industries available. Don't lose heart, we eventually returned to all these disqualified prospects after being able to prove RDS worked for them as well.

Once applied to a company's specific needs, every aspect of RDS reacts to and feeds another part. The logical, linked approach is why most non-salespeople, those typically detail -oriented, quickly embrace this rational approach. Because it is different, we caution the traditionally conservative and/ or highly structured organizations not to reach for RDS results without first firmly committing to properly executing the fundamental aspects of RDS. It was easier to quickly disqualify those who could not execute RDS than it was to know who was willing to adopt it and re-engineer their approach to internal resources and customers.

So which industries were targeted for quick success? We eagerly promote the application of RDS to individuals and organizations with complex, technical products and/or

We eagerly promote the application of RDS to individuals and organizations with complex, technical products and/or services.

> *The resource involvement of RDS means that no one individual can or should own a customer relationship.*

services. Additionally, it is very beneficial to those struggling with direct sales or distribution channel sales approaches that simply are not maintaining or growing revenue. We also considered organizations experiencing a general lack of teamwork between sales, marketing, operations, finance and the other disciplines in proactively servicing and securing customers. After filtering through our prospects, we secured a somewhat diverse group of clients, including government economic development, tool and die, food processing, institutional pharmacy and various service companies.

It may sound crazy, but before any company considers risking or investing in an approach that will lower costs, shorten the sales cycle and significantly increase customer satisfaction, growth and retention, the leaders must first defy their own instincts and overcome the fear that their business will suffer without old school salespeople. In fact, one of the first counter-intuitive decisions a management team must make before evaluating RDS is to be prepared to look at their internal resources differently. Additionally, management must be willing to put non-traditional resources face-to-face with customers. If the statement, "people do business with people" is interpreted to mean, "salespeople own customer relationships," RDS is not likely to work. The resource involvement of RDS means that no one individual can or should own a customer relationship. People do business with people, but not solely with a single

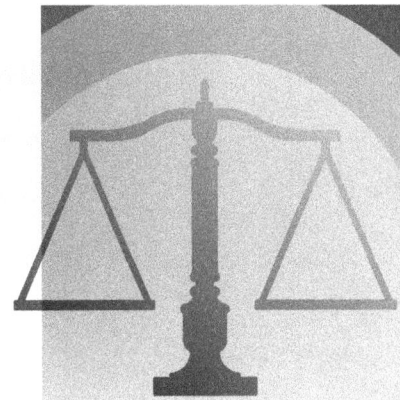

person. We believe that people do business with companies who allow their employees to solve problems and earn trust.

Many years ago I was hired by a venture capitalist to be the CEO of a 115-year-old business with deep-rooted issues. The company had been family owned for generations until being sold to the venture capitalists. Within weeks of my arrival I realized that Paul, the number one salesperson, was a complete idiot. He was a card-carrying moron, incapable of executing this or any process. When I learned that Paul did 100% of his "dialing for dollars" from his phone in the office and seldom dealt face-to-face with our customers, I decided to dig a little deeper. I listened to Paul dial for his commission dollars and heard him pressure customers into placing orders early so he could make his monthly commission. He begged, pleaded and even demanded orders for his own personal benefit. Paul was only 33 years old, but somehow managed to deploy his unprofessional tactics for 10 years. At that time, Paul consistently delivered 40% of our company's revenue month in and month out. Because our company specialized in exotic products I assume the customers allowed Paul to pressure them for orders because they felt we were the only game in town. The Internet was gaining momentum and the options were soon to become more apparent, but for then, Paul appeared to hold his customers hostage. I imagine if Paul were attempting this same approach today his failure

> *We believe that people do business with companies who allow their employees to solve problems and earn trust.*

would be significantly accelerated.

I saw absolutely no value in Paul so I announced to my senior staff that we needed to terminate him and assign his accounts to the other resources. My staff was terrified and warned me that if our number one salesperson was released, we would risk losing a big piece of our revenue. I told them I was willing to risk it all, but that I didn't feel we'd lose anything if we planned accordingly. We developed a plan to shore things up prior to terminating our so-called superstar. We divided Paul's customer list into three categories: A, B and C. The A's were the biggest revenue customers and in addition to a planned phone call by a designated resource, I also called the president or owner and assure them that the change in personnel would be seamless. The B's and C's also had customer service, operations and billing resources designated to call various contacts within each organization. Our plan was not just assuring a seamless transition, but delivering improved communication and service so that Paul would never be missed.

We rolled our transition plan out to our resource team at the same time the Sales VP was terminating Paul. The entire team lit up the phones before Paul was even out of the building. The first unexpected result was not a single customer voiced any concern. That gave the non-sales resources an extra shot of confidence to continue to call

and service the customers. Next, we executed a plan to over communicate and follow up at all levels with a three phase high customer touch approach plan of face-to-face visits, phone calls and written correspondence. These extra touches actually generated encouraging feedback that service had improved since Paul left, which in turn led to boosted morale and resource confidence. Bottom line, our penetration with Paul's customers actually increased because our team of resources proved that they had easily out-serviced one very over-rated, self-important old school salesperson. The internal fear of the unknown proved to be much, much greater than the actual reaction of the customer base.

Before making any organizational adjustments, all of the resources need to be objectively assessed. For twenty years I gave and received annual performance assessments and although I want to believe most centered on positive attributes and accomplishments, I can recall nearly every one ending with a list of two or three areas that needed to improve. That's the way performance appraisals are generally designed. Highlight positives, but close with a list of things to correct or improve. Based on appraisals I have given and received over the years, I also know that the sting of what needs to improve outlasts the brief ecstasy of being told what was done well.

> *The internal fear of the unknown proved to be much, much greater than the actual reaction of the customer base.*

CORE ELEMENT 3

Assess and Capitalize on Resource Strengths

Everyone has an inner brilliance just waiting to be revealed. A simple behavioral assessment (similar to DISC) will identify those inner skills, strengths and attributes. Blending resource strengths minimizes the individual weaknesses and accomplishes much more than risking personality conflicts by deploying the same person every time.

The counter-intuitive lesson we took from performance appraisals became the third Core Element contained in RDS. Disregard the traditional appraisal process and look only for strong natural attributes rather than ways to change weaknesses into strengths. What is the best way to assess those strengths and behavioral styles? There are a number of behavioral style assessments available, but we like the ten-minute on-line DISC (Dominant, Interactive, Steady, Compliant) assessment for its accuracy as well as the instant printable report available to both the individual and his/her supervisor.

DISC can provide a fundamental understanding of internal resource and external customer behavioral styles. Because of the complexity of the human personality, we do not suggest an assessment be used to simplify or compartmentalize any human being. That being said, in general, most Dominants focus on results, control, power and being respected. Many Interactives focus on influencing, persuading and like to be socially accepted. For a Steady, the focus is on logical, step-by-step processes and loyalty to a trusted inner circle. Compliants long for accuracy and precision. Although we strongly endorse utilizing a behavioral style assessment, we caution not to approach it as a strict rule. In RDS, it is used as a guideline for balancing and planning. What's more, no one style is better than another and all have a significant role in RDS.

Historically, most performance review discussions are intentionally discreet and keep all aspects of the individual's strengths and weaknesses strictly confidential. The RDS approach challenges traditional business norms by openly sharing each individual's DISC style with the rest of their team. Both management and customer facing resources share their style attributes and shortcomings with a special emphasis on highlighting their strengths. For instance, Compliant and Steady styles should share with the team their top of mind focus on process and accuracy, because they quite possibly have the natural technical skill to accurately anticipate and satisfy a customer's complex problem. However, they may not necessarily be comfortable initiating a conversation with a prospective customer. In RDS, the Compliant/Steady resource is encouraged to balance a talkative Dominant or Interactive associate on a customer visit by providing logic and detail. Understanding the behavioral styles of the entire resource team is a critical element in ensuring a balanced resource team.

Improved performance comes when motivated teams learn to harness and balance their collective strengths, then accommodate, work around, or shore up the weaknesses. How does one tolerate a customer service person with poor attention to detail and follow up, or a manager with the warmth and empathy of a pirate? Balance. No one is perfect and no one person can execute everything flawlessly. The

> *Understanding the behavioral styles of the entire resource team is a critical element in ensuring a balanced resource team.*

> *The very things most of us do not want to admit, let alone share, are the very strengths and weaknesses the resource team must learn.*

reverse is also true; no one has zero value or is incapable of contributing something to the team. Therefore, resource teams who understand each other's strengths and shortcomings can cover for each other and help balance one another. Most groups fail to balance, gel and cover for each other because they are too busy covering their individual proverbial behinds, blaming others for botched efforts, or simply learning how to avoid or sabotage a salesperson who they perceive took the credit once again. Over time, this pattern of distrust and resentment builds and as it does, the miscommunication, distrust and lack of teamwork grows until little is left except towering departmental silos. When that happens, a unique, but effective way to dismantle years of silo building is to do what most will say feels uncomfortable and counter-intuitive – that is to invite all of the cross functional resources together to share their most guarded fears, failures and strengths. The very things most of us do not want to admit, let alone share, are the very strengths and weaknesses the resource team must learn to communicate and then balance. Most of us will eventually share if the sharing is lighthearted, fun and serves a purpose. Great teams throughout history such as the 1980 US Men's Hockey team were not necessarily the most talented, or even best in class. However, they defied the odds by working together and relying on each other's strengths only after first identifying and covering for each other's weaknesses. That is why assessing and sharing a

team's make up is an essential first step.

For those of you who are fans of Star Trek II, RDS can be summed up in the words of Spock. "The needs of the many out weigh the needs of the few or the one." RDS results in more productive and self-motivated resource teams that perform best when balanced because they realize that alone they are limited, but the strengths of the united team out weigh the strengths of the few or the one individual. Balancing simply means identifying each individual's significant God-given strength and applying that individual to a task that best suits them and the team. Sharing behavioral style strengths and weaknesses inspires blended resource teams to cover each other's collective behinds rather than any one individual's behind. This "needs of the many" mindset enables RDS to begin in earnest.

Chapter 3 Highlights

1. Managers must first determine if they want to follow the crowd and their competitors or make a commitment to take a risk and change the way they earn, grow and retain customers.
2. Develop a plan to anticipate what your employees and customers will need to hear regarding the implementation to a RDS approach.
3. Change does not have to have a negative impact. Anticipate, plan and shore things up in advance. Good planning and planning for the unexpected will significantly decrease or eliminate a number of negative issues.
4. The third Core Element, *Assess and Capitalize on Resource Strengths,* involves helping resources assess their strengths, not their weaknesses. A natural tendency can be to judge based on assessed or observed weaknesses. However, doing so will only reinforce your reluctance to place non-sales resources in front of customers.
5. Find a behavioral assessment process like DISC that fits your organization. Have fun sharing, balancing and focusing on individual strengths that complement and cover for other individual styles.

Chapter 4 — Reengineering, Planning and Pipelines

CHAPTER SNAPSHOT
- Providing insight into reengineering organizational structure, cutting inefficiencies while increasing customer satisfaction
- Compelling resources to regularly track their plan, identify road-blocks and make adjustments to the strategy to increase the likelihood of delivering the corporate objective
- Utilizing pipelines to provide options and expose opportunities

After the resource team is assessed and balanced, the next step is to encourage resources to get directly involved in RDS planning and customer interactions. A common misconception is only salespeople can sell and that non-sales resources can be distracted from other important job responsibilities if they are expected to build customer relationships. Most salespeople are not tasked with delivering the services they sell so their words can fall short of customer expectations. As consumers, most of us have been on the receiving end of a salesperson's unfulfilled commitment. Typically, a non-sales resource is tasked with delivering on that salesperson's promises.

Customers generally trust those who deliver the product and/or service. Non-sales resources can generate trust by simply following through on their daily tasks, such as talking on the phone to customers, resolving billing issues,

> *A common misconception is only salespeople can sell and that non-sales resources can be distracted from other important job responsibilities if they are expected to build customer relationships.*

Management needs to provide structure and autonomy in order to allow the non-sales resources to create and execute a plan to strengthen customer relationships while still performing their everyday job functions.

providing technical support, delivering the product or providing product information. Developing prospective customers and providing service to current customers often cannot take place without non-sales resources. Most buyers want vendors who do what they say they will do, not old-style salespeople who sell, tell and promise. That can take a great deal of planning on the part of a blended resource team.

Many managers rely primarily on salespeople to maintain customer relationships because they underestimate non-sales resources' ability to sustain strong customer relationships. Management needs to provide structure and autonomy in order to allow non-sales resources to create and execute a plan to strengthen customer relationships while still performing their everyday job functions. However, although management should provide the resources with the means to achieve specific goals, it is very important that they trust that the resource team will find a way to actually achieve the goals. In other words, management presents "what" is expected but allows the resource team to decide "how" the goals are to be achieved. A major constraint can be time! Non-sales resources will initially struggle with prioritizing and managing both customer relationships and daily job responsibilities. Individuals gravitate toward the responsibilities they are most comfortable with and skilled in, and in many job

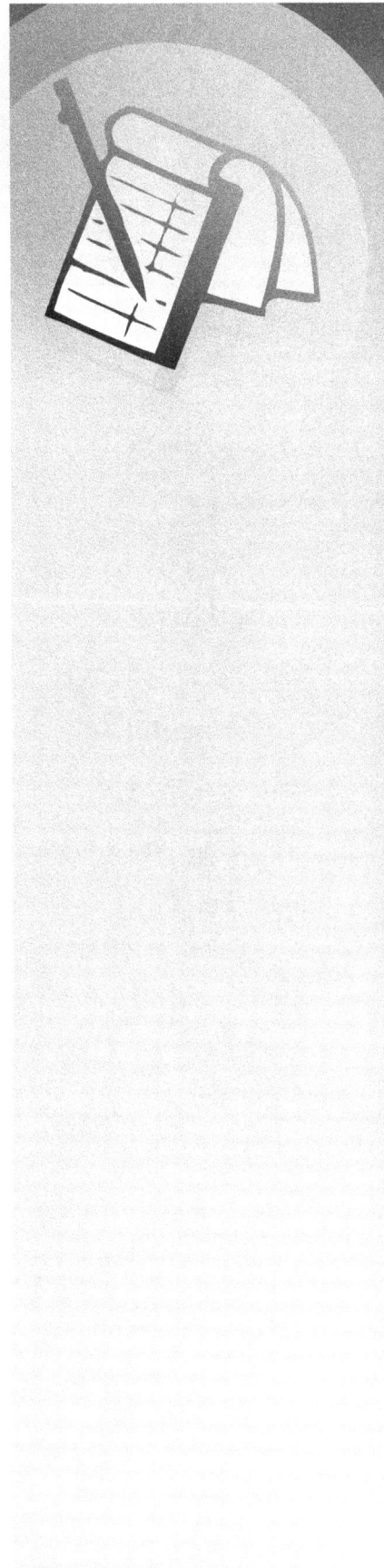

functions, communicating regularly with customers is nowhere near the top of the list. With securing customers as the main motivator for most salespeople, a "sales sense of urgency" drives salespeople to constantly think about the customer. Because they are paid for customer-facing efforts, many salespeople make the customer their greatest priority, regularly calling, following up and finding ways to make the customer happy. However, when a non-sales resource is asked to service a customer and maintain the relationship while doing their regular job, time becomes the biggest constraint. If time prohibits them from doing all things well, the sense of urgency demonstrated by non-sales resources is usually tied to their daily job responsibilities, which historically did not include selling. That explains why the customer is generally not a "priority" for non-salespeople to the extent it is for a salesperson, but that doesn't have to be the case. If time is the constraint that limits non-sales resource involvement with customers, management can solicit resource input on how they can create time to get more involved with customers.

In today's highly competitive business environment, many companies believe they have already trimmed the fat and are now cutting to the bone. Short-term cost reductions focused on scaling back operations and employees without considering some degree of reengineering may not create enough time, reduce enough costs, promote efficient work

> *RDS was not created to reduce costs, reengineer departmental structure, or cut fat – although it can do all three.*

flow, make for a more positive customer experience or foster teamwork. RDS was not created to reduce costs, reengineer departmental structure, or cut fat – although it can do all three. It was specifically designed to provide a competitive edge in growing and maintaining customers. However, RDS can provide the side benefit of a bottom-up, team designed, reengineering of the sales and service approach, reducing costs while increasing customer satisfaction and ultimately revenue.

With the short-term focus of corporate goals and the time constraints, it is natural to delay implementing any change in philosophy until a "better time." Out-of-the-box reengineering requires patience, commitment, resetting expectations and understanding that investing time today will save time tomorrow. Several years ago, while facilitating a public speaking session for a group of business professionals at a local university, one participant chose to speak on the topic of the fair tax. I must admit, up until that time I didn't give a consumption tax concept much thought, so this speech proved to be very enlightening for me. The participant spoke about the notion that a consumption tax would minimize the need for the IRS and most of the complex tax regulations. It would also lessen the need for tax attorneys and tax preparation assistance because the tax return may no longer be necessary. It would eliminate the need for hundreds of thousands of federal, state, local and private jobs in addition to streamlining an individual's taxes based primarily on the items and services consumed. I thought that a tax based on consumption made a lot of sense, not because it would affect my tax rate, but because theoretically it sounded like it could reduce a great deal of the cost, confusion and need for constantly changing and growing government regulations. I imagine that is exactly why special interest groups and our government may never consider it. But the lesson learned from this speech was if leadership is willing to blow up what has always been done and risk reengineering from scratch, an organization that thinks it has trimmed the fat can still do things more efficiently. For instance, one of our clients eliminated some salespeople and claims inspectors, reallocating many of those resources to operations and customer service areas. Reengineered efficiency, combined with a communal sales sense of urgency can boost confidence and create the time needed for non-sales resources to focus on customer relationships and trust building, as well as their current jobs. The only essential element one needs is a plan.

RDS relies on business plan trackers and strategies to help the resource team understand and achieve goals. Although the elements of what businesses track can vary, it is important to monitor the essential indicators with a simple, one-page summary that everyone has access to. For instance, a one-page business plan tracker can measure

> *The only essential element one needs is a plan.*

CORE ELEMENT 4

Create a Simple, One-Page Business Plan Tracker

Involving resources from the bottom up when setting and attaining goals can provide more insight, options and an increased likelihood of success. Jointly develop, track, execute, change and improve the team's tactical one page business plan on a regular basis to more effectively link accountability with the resources best suited to deliver the results.

target revenue, realized revenue and the variance between the two. Resource adjustments on "how" to address the variance become the plan. Most business plans contain the strategic and tactical steps required to meet a company's overall budget. They are usually rolled out once a year, contained in a nice binder, but generally end up on a shelf collecting dust. Intentions are good at the beginning of the year, but the document is either forgotten or rendered ineffective due to unanticipated market conditions throughout the year. The RDS plan is a very fluid approach to allow the resource team great flexibility in how the numbers are achieved. With RDS, the team's plan is still annual, but is tracked and adjusted at least monthly or in some cases, weekly by the team.

Because attaining revenue objectives is vital to nearly every organization, RDS utilizes a simple, one-page business plan tracker, our fourth Core Element. We suggest an easy-to-use document that tracks progress and provides clarity of vision for the team. Each month, the resource team evaluates the previous 30 days and year-to-date results, internal issues and external trends, then brainstorms what needs to be done at that moment in time to stay on course. It is much easier to make adjustments early when one recognizes a change in course is needed. Playing catch-up is a risky proposition, where bad decisions are often short-term knee jerk corrections that can lead to more corrections down the road. The closer the resources are to the front line, the more accurate and timely the information can be, allowing for early identification of roadblocks. Corrections can be made quickly, thus increasing the likelihood of achieving annual revenue objectives. Therefore, a simple one-page business plan tracker monitored by front line resources can locate and correct potential issues faster and more effectively than a formal business plan created and administered by high level management.

Traditional business planning tends to involve a top-down, hard target which many executives have backed into or seemingly assigned without much forethought other than to satisfy investor expectations. Although many understand and would welcome a common sense approach to generating a business plan from the bottom up, most companies, especially those that are publicly traded, give guidance from the highest level. They insist the rest of the organization find a way to "hit the numbers," utilizing plans that aren't plans at all, just numbers. Those numbers are seldom altered during the course of the year even if it is obvious they cannot be attained. However, resource teams who regularly discuss and plan how to achieve revenue goals tend to consistently deliver results because they are able to make adjustments and substitute other options throughout the year. Resource teams who measure activities (the means) that lead to goals (the end) should review their plan and

> *The closer the resources are to the front line, the more accurate and timely the information can be, allowing for early identification of roadblocks.*

> *Top-level management simply cannot experience, anticipate, or execute as nimbly as resource teams because they are generally far removed from the front line.*

make adjustments throughout the course of the year. Top-down, static, strategic and/or tactical steps imposed on an organization may negatively impact the front line resources actually expected to execute the steps. A simple one-page tracker monitored and executed by the resource team, that rolls up to a fluid, strategic plan at a higher level can be more effective than a top down edict, regardless of how well thought-out or intended.

Another advantage to the multi-discipline resource team approach, especially where silos exist, is the reconnaissance gathered from numerous sources and viewpoints. In other words, in RDS, the right blend of resources is crucial to brainstorming, taking risks and making the adjustments needed to achieve the desired business plan outcome. Top-level management simply cannot experience, anticipate, or execute as nimbly as resource teams because they are generally far removed from the front line.

Nearly everyone has some kind of business plan, some elaborate, others mental concepts tucked away in the mind of the entrepreneur. Some are nothing more than sales revenue bogies. Regardless of the complexity or lack of sophistication, every plan has numbers in the goal. I learned long ago that simply assigning a number to an individual or team does not mean the number will be achieved. I had a manager who would take on herculean revenue forecasts and divvy up the unrealistic number into smaller, equally unrealistic numbers and then assign a salesperson's name to each number. She slept well for a week or so until she heard from the very people she assigned the numbers to that it was impossible to achieve the targets. Business plan numbers are "what" is expected, but "who" is involved and "how" they plan to achieve the numbers can be much more important. Business plans consist of numbers, but numbers alone cannot ensure that goals will be achieved.

Let's compare the numbers in a business plan to a GPS in a car. What is great about a GPS is it tracks progression and calculates the miles and the time remaining for your predetermined route, a very helpful tool. But after using the GPS on a few trips, it can become downright annoying if the driver chooses to deviate from the calculated fixed route. Most GPS units will recalculate or tell you to take a u-turn in order to go back to the original plan if you deviate at all. I have experienced business plans that were so cumbersome and detailed that management became resistant when I actually thought for myself, took a risk and attempted to deviate from the business plan. One misguided manager essentially asked me to take a u-turn and execute the organization's original plan that was clearly not working. In those days I was not as subdued and respectful as I am now, so I shared my opinion with a lot less tact and political sensitivity. Because I didn't do exactly what he asked me to

> *Business plans consist of numbers, but numbers alone cannot ensure that goals will be achieved.*

" I now have a fixed route and a designated time to which I am expected to adhere, regardless of potential influences that affect my plan. "

do, but was unable to do all of what I thought was right, the results were mixed and some opportunities were lost. Business plans and GPS units are meant to aid and guide, but not replace thinking or stifle well-planned changes in direction. When unforeseen roadblocks get in the way, old-fashioned thinking can provide flexibility and options.

As if it has a pulse, the GPS unit often assumes it has taken over. Not just the trip plan, but also the thinking and on-the-fly adjustments most of us make while traveling. What frustrates me most is once I enter the destination; the GPS calculates an arrival time, which then gets recalculated every time I deviate from the original plan. I am reminded repeatedly that I am not performing what the GPS initially planned. I now have a fixed route and a designated time to which I am expected to adhere, regardless of the potential influences that affect my plan. For the duration of my trip, I am reminded that I am behind schedule and deviating from the plan. When I stop for a bathroom or lunch break I find that I'm rushing my family along, forcing them to eat in the car or hold their natural biological needs for a more convenient time, all in an effort to satisfy a GPS unit just so I can achieve a plan that I never created. Even though I had no input into the GPS's estimated time of arrival, the short diversion of a bathroom break causes me to do everything in my power to catch up to that original arrival time the GPS laid out from the start of my trip, even if it means speeding.

Generally, management puts a great deal of effort into planning the annual business plan. However, too often the result of their effort comes across as "The Plan," a carved in stone, stagnant, 12 month edict. A stagnant or flexible business plan by itself, with or without tracking, does not always provide enough guidance for a team to achieve annual revenue targets. Options and alternatives can ensure the successful outcome of a plan, not the plan alone. A GPS can choose the most direct route, but take travelers on a path through obscure towns like the town where the movie Deliverance was filmed. Also, a GPS can fall victim to miles of highway construction with no options or alternatives. In business, often the most effective options and alternatives come from resource-managed customer pipelines. Pipelines that contain prospective customers allow the resource team to achieve revenue goals despite unexpected lost customers or demands that stretch and break the original budgeted expectations. Pipelines, the fifth Core Element, provide options when stringent business plans must change for any number of good reasons. A typical pipeline simply lists all prospective customers. The customers are then prioritized in order of importance and probability of a quick or likely close. Additionally, most pipelines include available revenue and the resources assigned to qualify or disqualify the potential customers.

Pipelines are absolutely essential because they allow

CORE ELEMENT 5

Utilize Pipelines

Creating a growth pipeline that lists potential customers and a retention pipeline that lists current customers can provide the resource team with the ability to prioritize and manage the field of target prospects and customers more efficiently and consistently. A regular review of each pipeline with appropriate resources keeps customer communication and solving customer problems the priority.

> *Pipelines are absolutely essential because they allow the resource team to prioritize their options and expose opportunities.*

the resource team to prioritize their options and expose opportunities they are capable of closing. They also can cut through the smokescreen of old school salespeople. This step can provide a boost of confidence for managers still reluctant to turn the task of growing and maintaining customers over to a balanced and blended team of non-sales resources.

Several years ago we had a client by the name of Norm. He was the proud owner of a flour mill, preparing to celebrate over 75 years in business. Faced with the possibility of losing his family's business due to difficulty in meeting his bank obligation, Norm asked for our help in getting his line of credit extended for six months in order to create some breathing room. We assessed his business, resources and leadership team, looking for any obvious solutions to immediately boost revenue and generate a profit and/or positive cash flow so the bank would extend a longer-term line of credit. Norm was a cross between the absent minded professor and the lovable Mr. Rogers, minus the annoying puppets, ancient P.F. Flyers, and simpleton sweater. It was easy to become personally invested in Norm's success because he was perhaps the nicest person either of us had ever worked with. All we wanted to do was help him save his business and continue to provide for the employees he cared so much about. Norm admitted his current financial situation was 100% his fault and frequently

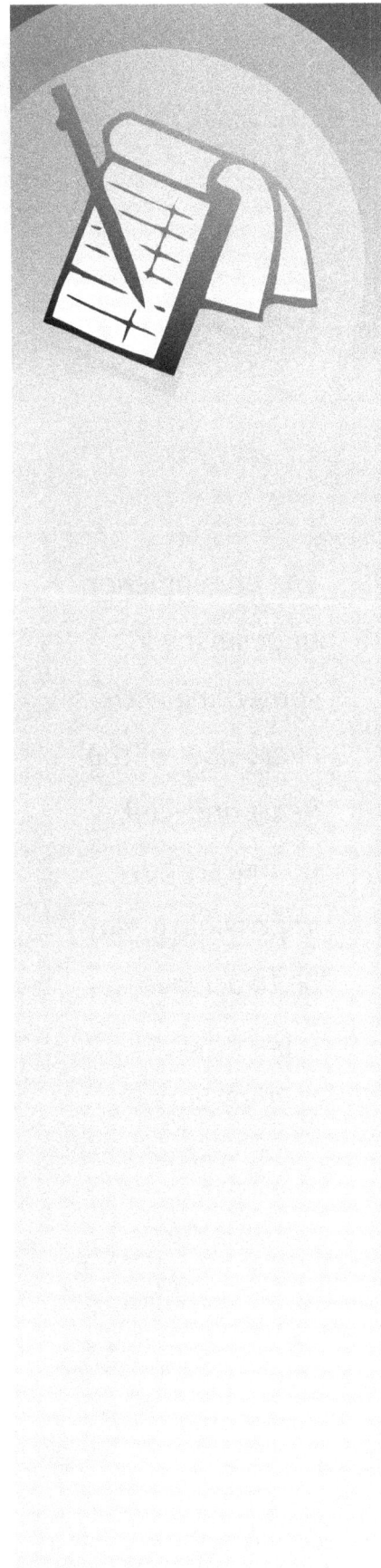

said and truly believed that, "The fish stinks from the head down." Although to this day I am not sure exactly what that saying means, it was clear that Norm's caring, trusting nature had resulted in frequent bad decisions and bad hires, mainly at the hands of those employees taking advantage of him. In fact, it was his inner circle of trusted confidants who were intentionally taking advantage of his trusting nature and bilking him out of hundreds of thousands of dollars. Norm was in serious trouble; he had sold vacation property, mortgaged his home and personally used his remaining assets as collateral on the loan he and his bank knew he could not repay.

Norm's new VP of Sales, Sam, one of the bamboozlers, was not only taking what little Norm had left, but was also providing Norm with the pretzel logic for decisions that were expediting the company's pending catastrophe. For instance, Sam openly angled for and received profit sharing despite the company's lack of profitability, convincing Norm that his sales team should be rewarded on gross revenue, not profit. Sam also hired independent manufacturer reps and told Norm it was standard practice to pay for their cars, expenses and medical benefits, and Norm naively went along with it.

In our very first meeting with Norm and the management team that January, Sam presented Norm with

> *The phenomenon of believing in something with every fiber of the heart and soul, no matter how impossible it may be to achieve is referred to as "Happy Ears."*

a sales forecast to take to the bank which was as ignorant as his profit sharing commission plan. Sam's bright idea was based on top line revenue and contained no costs, making us wonder if Sam even knew what profit actually meant. Sam's plan was to tell the bank that within five years, the small, local flour mill was going to become a national retail products company with a projected $100 million in sales. Chris and I did all we could do not to laugh, but sadly Norm bought into Sam's idea and started to craft the story for the conservative bankers.

The phenomenon of believing in something with every fiber of the heart and soul, no matter how impossible it may be to achieve is referred to as "Happy Ears." When I was eight years old, I had happy ears and still believed in Santa Claus even after my older brother told me Santa didn't exist. All of the evidence was there, even finding the presents my parents hid under the basement stairs, but I fought to believe that Santa was real. Both Sam and Norm wanted to believe that they could accomplish Sam's Santa-like story. Their confidence was so fervent that they started to convince themselves that simply because they wished to be a $100 million nationally recognized retail food brand, it could happen and therefore would happen. In an attempt to throw some cold water on a dim-witted idea, I jokingly suggested that such an accomplishment would not only extend the company's line of credit, but also would land the management team on the cover of Fortune, Time, Newsweek and perhaps even the National Enquirer. Sam and Norm agreed! I suddenly realized that we were meeting with the commanding generals over a confederacy of dunces! Chris and I knew Norm had no time for this kind of distraction so we asked Sam to provide a detailed forecast and pipeline of customers detailing his steps to the $100 million so we could include it in the detail for the upcoming bank meeting. The next request we had was for Norm's CFO to crunch the numbers and provide regular financial reports using weekly run rates and capacity utilization by workstation. The data requested was to be collected and summarized by the CFO but supplied by Bud the Production Manager.

While Sam, Norm and the CFO collected some additional data for us, Chris and I asked Bud for a 20-minute tour of the flour mill to better understand the operation. Although the tour did eventually prove to be beneficial, it began as a less than distinguishing moment for us. Before entering the flour mill operation, we had to cover our shoes with paper slippers and our hair with hair nets for sanitary reasons. The slippers made us look like elves, but it was cramming our hair into hair nets that invoked the most shame, especially since we failed to realize that the nets we mistakenly grabbed were intended for small beards, not a full head of hair. The mostly non-English speaking workers

> *I suddenly realized that we were meeting with the commanding generals over a confederacy of dunces!*

began pointing, laughing and muttering what appeared to be uncomplimentary sentiments in Spanish at the sight of two consultants sporting less than attractive hair buns on top of their heads. I knew something was wrong when I looked at Chris, who to me resembled Alice the maid from The Brady Bunch. When Chris stopped laughing, he snapped back something about me looking like Aunt Bea from The Andy Griffith Show. After collecting our composure and what remained of our dignity, we put on the much more flattering hair nets, took a tour, then returned to the management team to assure them our consultation would be more pertinent than our outdated woman's hairstyles.

Sam presented his forecast for the new calendar year, which projected the company to significantly increase sales revenue from the current run rate of $7.5 million to $20 million. Alarmingly, Sam's plan only took him 20 minutes to develop. It was full of customers they had never done business with, products that didn't yet exist and worst yet, 75% of Sam's total forecast was back-end loaded in the 4th quarter of the year. Chris and I recognized this old trick, used by fast talking old school salespeople who speak with confidence and buy time to find a way to hit their numbers. We agreed to arrange weekly pipeline reviews with Norm and Sam to drill down and list specific comments coming from these potential customers. Although our agreement was to facilitate their pipeline, our plan was really nothing

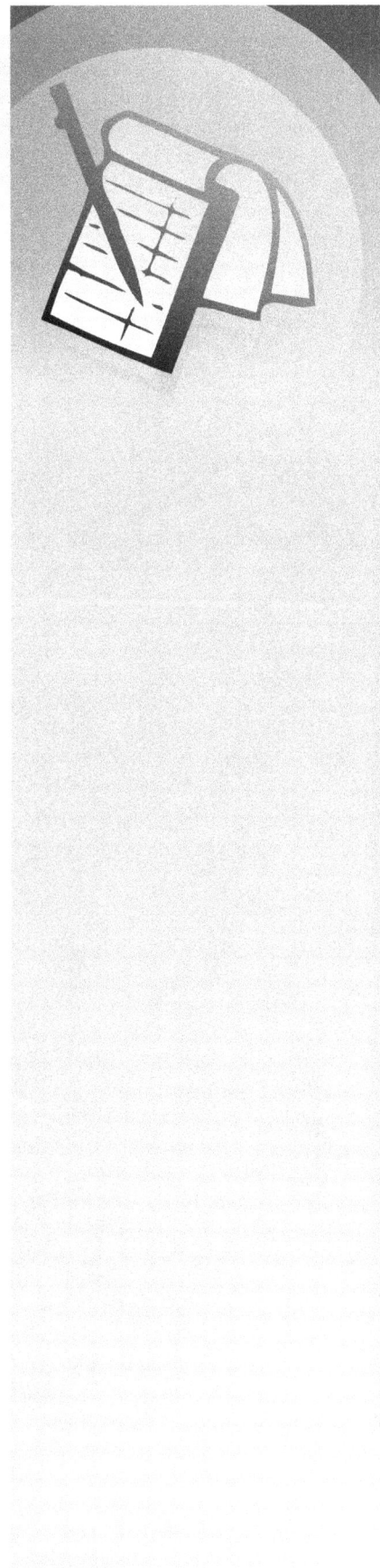

more than to provide enough rope for Sam to hang himself. The time had come to protect Norm by exposing Sam's manure. Even though we were not bankers or even skilled with balance sheets, we knew Norm's unproven plan would not persuade the bank to extend their line of credit. Bud provided the CFO with his run rates and costs and the CFO issued us weekly budgets detailing actual production, overhead and costs, deviations from budget and a summary snapshot of what the bank would see.

On the first pipeline review, Sam reported that he had issued very aggressive pricing to a $750 thousand a year prospective new customer who "really wanted to do business with the company." We noted his comments, documenting Sam's planned follow up was to drop off a contract that Friday. A side discussion with Norm and the CFO revealed that the aggressive pricing Sam offered was at least 10% below cost. The unprofitable company was actually planning to ask their bank for a credit extension so they could lose even more money on their customers; however, they would make it up in volume. What was worse was that this convoluted logic was the best that Norm's team had in response to the bank's threat to rescind their line of credit. Since that threat, Norm had hired us, the CFO and Sam the VP of Sales. Each of us was being compensated to help generate this stellar plan that was beginning to look as phony as an old Japanese Godzilla movie. If we hadn't already violated the number one rule to never become emotionally or personally attached to the client, we would have run out of that flour mill, paper shoes and hair nets in hand.

The following Monday, during our second pipeline review, Sam told us that he had a verbal commitment on the $750 thousand deal and that the customer really wanted to do business with him. When asked who made the verbal commitment and specifically about their decision-making process, Sam replied "This is a done deal; I pick up the contract Friday." That was good enough for Norm and the rest of the management team. Chris and I were skeptical of Sam's shallow declaration, a veiled undertaking to buy time and figure out how to deliver on his lofty assurances. It would be a matter of weeks before everyone realized the pile of dung Sam had served up.

The next week we asked Sam if he had picked up the contract. He said the contract was in legal review, but insisted it was still a done deal. As Sam focused most of his attention on talking his way in and around the $750 thousand deal, Chris and I managed to expose virtually all of Sam's targets classified as "done deals" on the pipeline as being even a lower probability than the $750 thousand done deal.

Norm finally began to see the benefit of the pipeline

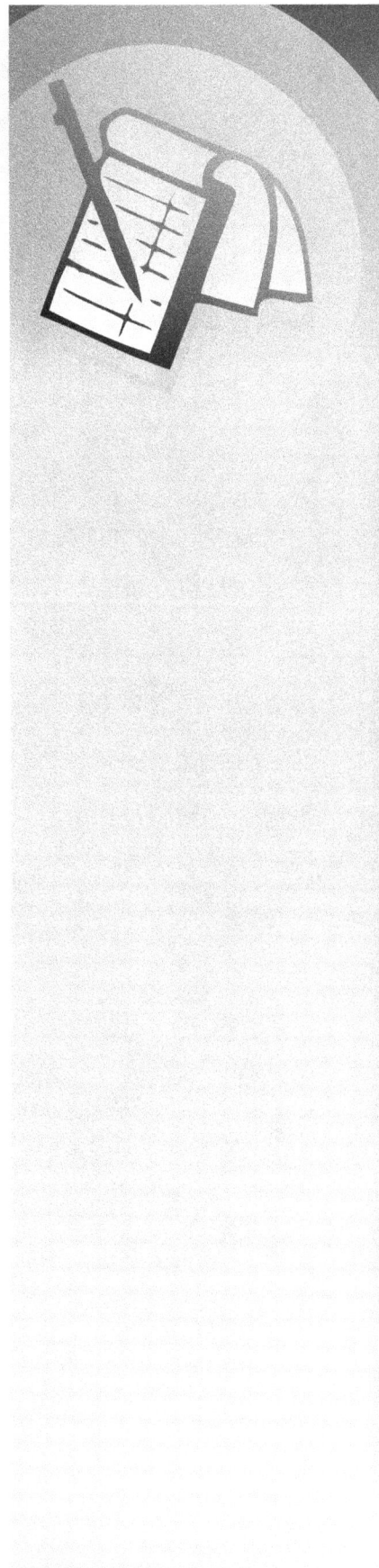

reviews and within those first few weeks, understood that the likelihood of actually securing $20 million that year was a function of Sam's happy ears, not of established customer interest. We were successful in getting Norm the credit extension with the bank, not based on Sam's sales forecast, but because of an observation we made during our tour of the flour mill. Norm had a massive piece of processing equipment that remained idle 90% of the time, even though he was incurring significant expenses on the capital expenditure made several years earlier. We suggested Norm maximize the use of his existing mixing equipment before considering any additional capital investment for their new product plan. Norm was able to negotiate a very lucrative short-term agreement with the U.S. Government, taking powdered milk and mixing it with protein for an overseas program to feed the poor. Within months, Norm's revenue went from a $7.5 million annual run rate to a $32 million run rate.

Norm was pleased with the outcome of our relationship but, because we were afraid of being sucked further into the confederacy of dunces, we chose to move on to other clients. Several years later we learned that Sam's $750 thousand "done deal" sat in legal review for nine months and he finally admitted to Norm that he didn't even know the customer's executive level decision makers and the real issues. Sam persevered and convinced Norm to invest in the

Growth pipelines provide options and show how big the breadbox of opportunity really is.

new retail food product development plan, a very expensive packaging line and warehouse, despite our previous advice not to do so. Our prior efforts to persuade Norm to let Sam go when he had the chance were obviously overruled by Sam's silver tongue. The last time we heard, Norm's sales fell to $10 million, he was deeply in debt with a different bank and he was desperately trying to sell homemade cakes, brownies and pancake packaged mixes to some of the biggest grocery chains in America. We continue to pray for Norm and the success of his company.

Growth pipelines provide options and show how big the breadbox of opportunity really is. They have the added benefit of forcing everyone, including old-style salespeople, to realize the true likelihood of success. Retention pipelines list every single current customer along with the potential risks of losing them. Pipelines alone are of no value until the team prioritizes how and when each opportunity will be explored. Regardless of what a GPS or business plan spells out, options can provide necessary alternatives that can and should be confidently made on the fly.

Chapter 4 Highlights

1. Commit to and make time available to plan a growth strategy. Provide several alternatives, since the best laid plans rarely mimic the actual outcome.

2. Implement the fourth Core Element, *Create a Simple One-Page Business Plan Tracker.* Involve resources at all levels in developing, tracking, executing, altering and improving the team's short term plan.

3. The fifth Core Element, *Utilize Pipelines*, is essential planning for both growth and retention. Growth pipelines should list every potential customer (possibly sourced from association directories, state business listings, industrial guides and employee knowledge). Retention pipelines list all current customers.

4. Don't mistake numbers to be the only goal in a business plan. The "how" of business plan achievement and the options available are as important if not more than the actual numbers themselves.

5. The closer resources are to the front line, the more nimble and proactive they can be in forecasting and achieving ever-changing revenue targets.

6. Many business plans, similar to a GPS-generated route suggest there is only one way to get to the results. That can often discourage the risk-taking creativity of blended resource teams.

7. Beware of "happy ears." Insist that RDS find and focus on the facts, not on what anyone thinks or hopes.

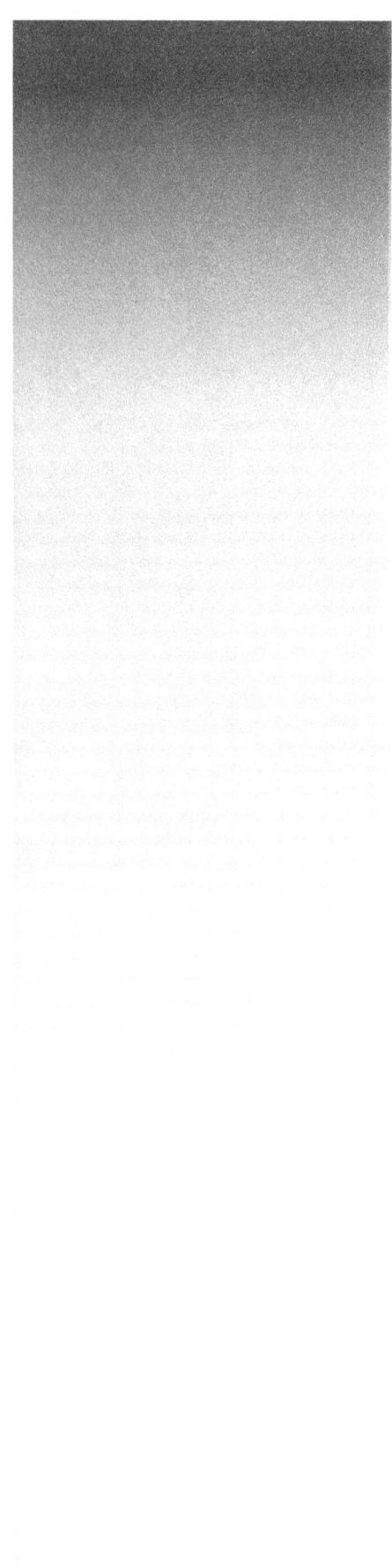

The Mechanics of RDS

5 Pipeline Probability Measures

CHAPTER SNAPSHOT
- Accurately measure and assess customer interactions by using a RDS pipeline probability scale
- Understanding the differences between the customer's decision-making approach and the seller's selling strategy

> *Disqualifying uninterested buyers can be a better use of time than attempting to qualify them.*

Although we've mentioned some pipeline applications, we need to start at the beginning. What exactly is a pipeline and what does it do? Traditional pipelines generally consist of a list of potential customers. Similarly, RDS pipelines also list potential customers but takes it a step further to quickly qualify or disqualify those prospects. Disqualifying uninterested buyers can be a better use of time than attempting to qualify them. For instance, if one loves to catch fish, knowing which ponds not to fish in because they seldom provide a catch can save valuable time to spend at well-stocked ponds. RDS pipelines are prioritized and prospects quickly disqualified in order to save time. The remaining qualified, high probability prospects remaining provide the RDS team with options for growth. Therefore, RDS pipelines can be a valuable source of revenue options.

Assembling a list of prospective customers provides the foundation for a systematic plan to sort those who have a high likelihood of becoming a customer from those with

> *A RDS pipeline prioritizes options and signals where a resource team should allocate their time.*

a low or no likelihood at all. Prioritization of customers is often subjective because it is always filtered through the individual company culture. For instance, some resource teams have a very simplistic and informal approach to their pipeline. They identify possible customers based on relationships with individuals they know. Others speculate based on rumors that suggest a prospect may be looking to change a current supplier. Some sort almost exclusively on potential revenue and presumed profitability. As long as targeting focuses disqualifying prospective customers for the right reasons, the lens through which the potential customers are scrutinized should be inconsequential.

After the target prospects are selected, what's next?

The next step is to objectively measure whether there is a solid fit with the prospect and if that fit can be expanded into a value for both parties. Measuring this can be accomplished by using a probability scale. An objective probability scale serves as the guide for the team's logical, step-by-step communications with various individuals involved in the prospective customer's decision-making process.

How do a pipeline and probability measurements interact? A RDS pipeline prioritizes options and signals where a resource team should allocate their time. A probability scale can provide a means of measuring the

Probability Scale Measurements

0% –	Unqualified
10% –	Contact made – Building relationship
20% –	Needs assessed and interest established
30% –	Internal champion identified
40% –	Decision-making process, players and behavioral styles identified
50% –	Trust established and player needs identified
60% –	Gained commitments from ALL players
70% –	Price, delivery and/or other terms identified
80% –	Negotiating agreements
90% –	Verbal agreement
100% –	Product/service delivery begins

progress of taking qualified pipeline prospects to satisfied new customers. The scale should realistically measure the resource team's effectiveness in building trust-based relationships and understanding and meeting the needs of the prospective customer.

A RDS probability scale is not a check-the-box, activity-based approach that simply documents actions. Some pipelines measure activities such as "initial contact made," the first "face-to-face visit" and "pricing provided," but these check-the-box activities can give the seller a false sense of security and therefore may not be objective or effective at assessing the true probability of success.

Players to Identify in the Decision-Making Process:

Approver - Signs or gives final authorization

Decision Maker - Makes the actual decision

Influencer - Gives input, positive or negative to anyone

Recommender - Gives their endorsement to the decision maker

User - Actually applies or benefits from the product or service

Blocker - Within or outside of the organization, can obstruct or completely derail a decision

Many old-style salespeople focus on their own selling process, commonly referred to as a sales cycle. This approach will often fail to take into account the buyer's perspective. For example, when a seller focuses on securing appointments to make product or pricing proposals the seller tends to view things from his own perspective and doing so generally results in "selling." However, if a seller resists selling and allows the buyer to buy, the seller will likely become a more successful sales organization. To increase chances of selling success, it can make more sense to track buyer-generated viewpoints and buying criteria than track sales cycle-based milestones.

RDS measures probability based on the steps of the Buyer's Stages of Buying (Chapter 9). The focus is building trust by asking, listening and learning the customer's wants and needs, not selling or promoting. Only after the trust is established can an internal customer "champion" guide the RDS team through the customer's decision-making process. It is imperative to accurately uncover and understand a customer's decision-making process before attempting to identify each individual or player (Approvers, Decision Makers, Influencers, Recommenders, Users and Blockers) involved in the decision process. In other words, find out how decisions are made as well as who is involved in making them. Once the decision-making process is clearly understood and the players properly identified, the resource team must address each of the decision maker's issues and concerns. A customer-centric probability scale, when objectively brainstormed and challenged through Negative Planning for Positive Results, reduces the harmful impact happy ears can have in creating inaccurate assumptions and disappointing failure. The importance of understanding the decision process and the players involved in the process cannot be stressed enough. Too many times have the resources we've dealt with told us "for a fact" how the decision-making process operates and who the decision makers are, only for us to find that a silent partner or another unknown but influential individual existed the entire time. In some instances the resources were out-maneuvered by the competition, who took the time to get it right. Tough questions must be asked and comfort zones temporarily disregarded to increase the chances of success.

So far, we've explained and established the pipeline list of prospective customers available and applied a probability scale from the buyer's viewpoint. The next step is to document the progress made in identifying and addressing the customer's needs through each step in the probability scale. Each communication between the resource team and the potential customer should be recorded and evaluated against the probability scale. The scale provides an objective means of measuring where the team stands in the buyer's stage of making a purchasing decision.

> *In some instances the resources were out-maneuvered by the competition, who took the time to get it right.*

The scale provides objective means of measuring where the team stands in the buyer's stage of making a purchasing decision.

A RDS pipeline should capture, summarize and measure all communication between the resource selling team and the buyer's team. Chronicling each customer interaction with specific names, dates and action steps helps the resource team sort out the difference between fact, speculation and the unknown, and guides the team in the appropriate direction. When properly captured, the comments read like a history book, revealing who said what, when it happened and next action to be taken. This history book reveals the past, but also leads the team closer to the goal of continuous movement up the probability scale. To illustrate, let's take prospective customer ABC, currently ranked at 0% because virtually nothing is known about them. After several phone calls, the probability rating moves to 10% as a relationship is being built. Additional contact quickly reveals interest and a need and moves ABC to 20% on the probability scale. In order to move to 30%, the team plans more contact with ABC to establish a stronger relationship with an individual who can help champion their effort. Recent comments documented in the pipeline confirm we have an inside contact advising our resource team on what needs to be done and with whom they need to meet. This inside track is the springboard to identifying the decision-making process and all of the players and their issues. Although it may sound like an endless cycle of call reports and data entry, it is not as strenuous is it seems. Many organizations utilize software programs to track customer communications. For others, simple Excel spreadsheets can capture pertinent details such as dates, people involved, comments and follow up.

Many people ask how long it should take for a prospect to move from 0% to 100%. Because time is not an accurate unit of measurement for building customer trust and confidence, it is very difficult to predict the time frame. Depending on the product and/or service, Buyer's Stage of Buying, urgency of the need and effective planning utilizing the buyer's behavioral styles, the buying cycle can be relatively quick or protracted. However, the unit of measurement to apply is not time but the pipeline probability scale itself. The quality of the steps taken, the strength of the relationships built and the strategy planned for each individual customer approver, decision maker, influencer, recommender, user and blocker, all documented in the comments section of the pipeline, are more accurate predictors of "how long" than any other measurement. The team must also be prepared to deal with the impact change can have on the probability scale as well. Changes in personnel or responsibility on the seller's team and/or the customer's team can impede relationships. Changes in the marketplace, regulations and unfavorable publicity can adversely impact movement on the scale, sending both buyer and seller a few steps back.

> *The team must also be prepared to deal with the impact change can have on the probability scale as well.*

> *Confidence, or the lack of confidence, is contagious and impacts both parties.*

Mutual trust is essential to promoting confidence in the buying/selling relationship. Confidence, or the lack of confidence, is contagious and impacts both parties. When the resource team is confident in themselves, they project that assurance which can instill a degree of trust in the buyer. Nearly anyone on the resource team (especially non-sales resources) can accomplish trust by planning and asking just one simple, closed-ended question to start the dialogue with a prospect. We've seen the question "Are you completely satisfied with your current supplier or are there things you'd like to see them do differently?" spark a flood of unfulfilled customer needs/wants. Identifying wants and needs can move the team to the 20% mark in the first meeting. A well-planned follow up question like "What would you suggest we do to be considered as a potential supplier?" could move the team to 30% by developing an internal champion, willing and able to guide the team through the decision-making process. Most RDS teams can quickly get to 30% in one or two customer discussions, but identifying the decision-making process, players and their individual needs and concerns can take a great deal of time and effort.

If the resource team can't get to 20% on the probability scale within a few weeks, they should consider deeming the prospect as a low probability of a fairly quick close. Like the mega grocery distributor Chris and I approached, classifying someone as a low probability simply means that either the buyer is not ready to buy, the seller's perceived value is unacceptable or the seller has not yet earned enough trust. In any case, a low probability prospect still deserves occasional communication from resource members to build a long-term, trust-based relationship at the buyer's pace. This allows the resource team to shift their short-term energy and efforts toward qualifying higher probability prospects.

If a pipeline report accurately captures comments, activities and action items from the customer's viewpoint and objectively guides the resource team through the RDS approach, the team will succeed in building customer confidence and trust. It is the mutual trust that will lead to a much higher likelihood of finding and keeping customers. We often tell our clients that buyers buy when they have a need and when they trust the seller. If a buyer does not have a need, a seller cannot create a need. However, if the buyer has an unrecognized need, the seller may be able to help the buyer realize that need. RDS resources take the time to develop relationships that lead to trust. If there is no need and selling continues, a prospect can become frustrated and lose confidence in the seller. However, if a buyer has a trust-based relationship with a non-pushy seller, the buyer will more likely buy from this trusted resource when a need finally arises.

> *If a buyer does not have a need, a seller cannot create a need. However, if the buyer has an unrecognized need, the seller may be able to help the buyer realize that need.*

"A Tale of Two Deals" will illustrate how the probability scale can help to qualify and disqualify. These two pursuits are an illustration of the impact the probability scale can have on accurately predicting whether efforts will succeed or not.

Our first tale involves Ginny, a salesperson for a professional services firm. Ginny had verbal approval on what she classified as a "done deal" and needed a little assistance just pushing it over the finish line. When Ginny saw the pipeline scale, she determined that her pursuit was at 90%. Like a recurring bad dream, hearing the words "done deal" immediately put us in Negative Planning mode and we challenged Ginny on her 90% rating.

Our initial task was to confirm that the proposal had indeed been reviewed and that pricing met expectations. When we inquired on the pricing/proposal status, Ginny told us that her corporate group did not yet finalize the pricing. That statement was strange and raised a red flag. How could she have gotten a verbal approval when neither the pricing nor the agreement was in her possession? We referenced the probability scale and broke the news to Ginny that she was in fact, not at 90%, but likely at 70%. We assured her that this was not a negative reflection of her efforts, just a realistic, conservative assessment to truly understand where we stood.

After a few days, Ginny learned the Vice President of Operations at the prospective client was going to make the final decision. We asked her what the VP of Ops needed or wanted in a professional services firm. Sheepishly, Ginny confessed she didn't know because she had never met the VP of Ops. Of course, that meant that once again we'd bear more bad news to Ginny. Ginny's prospective deal was not at 70%, since she hadn't received the commitment of all the decision makers, it was down to 60%. However, without any relationship with the VP of Ops, Ginny's opportunity was 40% at best. She had some work to do to initiate a relationship with the VP and uncover what he needed. Since Ginny did have an internal champion, we settled with the fact that Ginny's opportunity was realistically 30%, a far cry from the 90% she had initially proclaimed.

Unfortunately Ginny told her management that this opportunity was a "done deal," increasing her management's confidence to forecast revenue. Before revealing the outcome, let's look at deal number two in the Tale of Two Deals.

The second example begins with a team at a small manufacturing facility who had an astounding lack of information regarding a prospective customer, bringing them to the assumption that this was a low to no probability prospect. The resource team had only one remote point

Probability Scale Measurements

- 0% – Unqualified
- 10% – Contact made – Building relationship
- 20% – Needs assessed and interest established
- 30% – Internal champion identified
- 40% – Decision-making process, players and behavioral styles identified
- 50% – Trust established and player needs identified
- 60% – Gained commitments from ALL players
- 70% – Price, delivery and/or other terms identified
- 80% – Negotiating agreements
- 90% – Verbal agreement
- 100% – Product/service delivery begins

of contact, a District Manager and the team was unsure if there was even a need. We generously started at 10% on the probability scale while they built the relationship. The team was a blended team, but since this prospect was such a low probability, the salesperson didn't even get involved. The resource team, led by a product engineer named Doug, planned their first meeting and created a call plan with objectives and questions intended to qualify or disqualify the prospect. They met with the District Manager, and after asking the planned questions, the team learned that their prospect might have a need, and proceeded to identify the decision process. Instead of asking the District Manager if he was the decision maker, they asked, "What process do you go through when making a decision for a project of this nature?" If the team had not asked the District Manager about the decision-making process itself, the team's intelligence gathering process could have stopped. Had the District Manager claimed he was the decision maker, whether his statement was true or not, it would make it very difficult to go over his head to meet and build trust with others.

At this point, the team determined they were at 30% because they had identified a champion, understood the decision-making process and began to uncover most of the needs. In a matter of weeks, the resources team met with several higher level decision makers where more needs were uncovered. As time went on, the team was able to better understand the prospect's needs and develop customized solutions. Since the solution was created with the input of the buyer, no other provider could touch the final package. This deal quickly jumped from 40% to 50% to 80% since the team was negotiating the procedures and associated costs during their interactions. They didn't throw a proposal over the wall hoping for the prospect to accept it, instead they built a proposal as they built a trusting, long-term customer.

How do pipeline probability scales help qualify and disqualify? The Tale of Two Deals demonstrates it very well.

Deal number one never happened. Ginny's management continued to forecast the revenue for one more month until they too realized their "done deal" was a dead deal. Deal number two signed a three-year, multi-million dollar contract.

> *They didn't throw a proposal over the wall hoping for the prospect to accept it, instead they built a proposal as they built a trusting, long-term customer.*

Chapter 5 Highlights

1. Objectively measure the probability of securing a customer.
2. Measure progress on a probability scale by focusing on building mutual understanding and trust with the prospect.
3. Clearly defining the prospect's decision-making process prior to attempting to identify all of the players will switch the focus from people to process, thus avoiding happy ears and a strategy that misses the mark.
4. Identify the concerns, needs and preconceived opinions of each and every
   - a. Approver
   - b. Decision Maker
   - c. Influencer
   - d. Recommender
   - e. User
   - f. Blocker
5. Chronicle each customer interaction with specific names, dates and action steps.
6. Qualifying and securing a new customer can happen as rapidly as disqualifying a low probability pursuit. In either case, the value is in quickly knowing where the team stands.

Chapter 6 — Customers & Companies Have No Needs

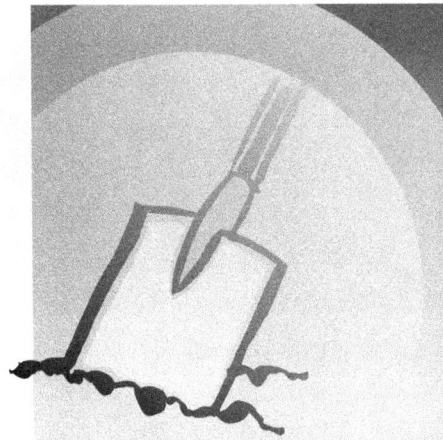

CHAPTER SNAPSHOT

• Targeting all individuals in an organization using questions, not assumptions

• Avoiding disqualification by understanding all players in the decision-making process, including the individuals, known or unknown, who can torpedo the best planned sales strategy

The fear of selling is often the consequence of misunderstanding the buyer's buying process which leads to errors in judgment and even failure, further augmenting the fear of selling. One major mistake many salespeople make is they consider the prospective customer a single entity, as the "company" or the "customer." Even good salespeople who make an effort to address a customer's issues, needs and concerns can assume that one well-researched, universal pitch or approach can cover all the bases. However, that type of approach cannot be successful because the "company" can have no issues, needs, concerns, or feelings since the company itself is nothing more than a building housing individual people. Obviously, people make up a company and those individual people have a variety of separate and unique issues, needs, concerns and feelings that, if addressed individually, can generate ample confidence and trust to at least continue a dialogue with the seller.

> *Instead of a pitch, RDS focuses on brainstorming separate strategies and questions for each customer's behavioral style (DISC) and job responsibility.*

When the seller addresses "the customer" with a single approach, it almost always misses the mark. Many salespeople use a "one size fits all" approach with multiple individuals within one prospective target, expecting to succeed. What a colossal waste of time! Instead of a pitch, RDS focuses on brainstorming separate strategies and questions for each customer's behavioral style (DISC) and job responsibility.

For example, an area florist wants/needs a new truck to deliver their floral arrangements. The seller researches the company and learns that they are growing and now servicing a much larger 300 square mile area. He creates a logical proposal for the buyer: to buy a new, significantly larger refrigerated truck with a fuel tank that will allow for longer routes. The presentation is well researched and therefore sounds reasonable, so the single dimension approach is delivered to a room full of decision makers.

The owner of the floral company is a fast-paced risk taker who has a tendency to make quick decisions, over commit and leave his team struggling to deliver on his commitments and expectations. The sales pitch sounds great to the owner and he is ready to buy the truck and get sales revenue growing again. The seller thinks he has hit a home run, but underestimates the impact his approach has on the behavioral styles of the other individuals still waiting

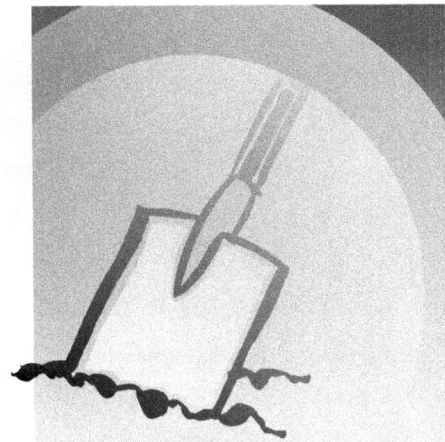

to be convinced that the new large truck is the best solution. These individuals have different job responsibilities and measurements driving their decision process. The detail-oriented finance guy has already conspired with the very conservative purchasing manager and now they wait for the owner to leave the room before informing the seller that they will fight tooth and nail against this single, large truck solution. The seller never asks, so the very influential purchasing and finance team's objections are not voiced, but they won't endorse any decision until they have an opportunity to analyze projected maintenance costs, fuel economy ratings and lease versus purchase options. They are not comfortable with the seller because he just made their job more difficult with their boss. They are weeks away from making a decision.

The sales manager, a ready-shoot-aim kind of person wants multiple trucks so he can plaster them with images of the company's products and phone number in order to increase sales interest. He blurts out without being asked that he doesn't want anything to do with the seller's big white truck. In fact, his suggestion is to purchase a couple of smaller trucks with colorful graphics plastered all over them. The finance and purchasing folks support that idea because smaller trucks might meet their budget requirements. The delivery drivers' opinions have not yet been shared. Prior to the meeting, they already discussed their concerns of maneuverability, comfort and a desire for shorter delivery routes, and they too buy into the option of a fleet of smaller trucks covering more frequent, yet shorter routes. The operations manager ends the meeting with a comment that delivery would be dramatically improved with more trucks and shortened runs.

Our seller finds himself among a somewhat hostile group of influencers and users, and after successfully selling the owner, he very likely sabotaged his own efforts by alienating the rest of the players in the decision-making process. This happened despite his well-researched single approach, which he now realized completely missed the mark for every one except the owner. The likelihood of being able to earn the team's trust has decreased dramatically and therefore, he will likely fail to sell the "company" he so carefully targeted.

For non-sales resources, failing to prepare and falling short of the expectation of securing a sale can be enough to ignite a fear of selling. This fear can prevent the resources from having a desire to participate in regular customer communication in the future. RDS strives to prevent perceived failures, especially as non-sales resources begin to participate. Recognizing that each individual must be handled separately, although initially requiring more preparation and effort, can actually minimize the odds of failure and boost a non-sales resource's confidence.

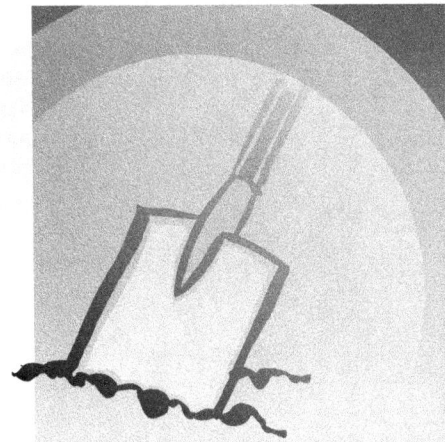

Understanding the entire decision-making process and identifying more than just the obvious individuals involved in the decision are by far the most frequently underestimated and underdeveloped critical elements even the most experienced sales professionals miss. This lack of knowledge and attention can severely reduce the odds of successfully developing new customers. With the RDS approach, all levels of the buying organization are targeted (Executives, Middle Management, Lower Level Supervisors/Employees) and no one is taken for granted. We've seen potential deals fail at the hands of low-level users and mid-level recommenders who sabotaged efforts simply because they were overlooked or ignored. Sometimes it's been the obscure high-level approvers who quietly developed options with other suppliers. If any of the levels are not properly identified, understood and serviced, the end result can be devastating.

It only takes one individual on the buying team to push back on changing suppliers by either sending the buying team in a different direction or stopping progress altogether. That single occurrence of doubt from one blocker can become a cancer that starts the politicking against changing suppliers altogether. Although it can take a great deal of time to expose every individual's issues, needs and concerns, it can be more effective for non-sales resources than old-style salespeople. Non-sales resources generally tend to

> *We've seen potential deals fail at the hands of low-level users and mid-level recommenders who sabotaged efforts simply because they were overlooked or ignored.*

> *Questions expose needs and issues, both of which, if not uncovered and addressed can be damaging or even deal breaking.*

ask more than tell because they assume little and want to learn. Old-style salespeople confidently tell and sell and therefore can fail to ask as many questions. Questions expose needs and issues, both of which, if not uncovered and addressed can be damaging or even deal breaking. If a blocker has issues, uncovering those issues early will at the very least prevent an ambush and save both parties a great deal of time. Negative Planning those potentially damaging issues through well-prepared questions will get the team to a "No" or "Yes" more efficiently than an old-style sales "pitch" inclusive of presentations, promotion of features and/or price. Asking questions focuses the team's effort in the customer's direction and potential customers who have a need and interest present a higher likelihood of success. Questions can also quickly dispel erroneous initial assumptions and can prevent the resource team from making decisions, statements and forecasts based on happy ears, hope, or hearsay.

Chapter 6 Highlights

1. Beware of the broad, single approach, hoping that something will "stick."
2. Identify all levels of the buying organization, including Executives, Middle Management and Lower Level Supervisors/Employees.
3. Take the time to prepare questions, strategies and responses for each and every individual in the decision-making process.
4. The individuals in the company, not the company itself, make the decision. The behavioral styles are as numerous as the options for which the team may have to prepare. A single, overall strategy may be appropriate, however, the approach needs to be adjusted for each individual.
5. Asking questions and seeking input in creating solutions vs. predetermining and assuming the solution, reduces the risk of alienating individuals and fosters joint exploration of a win-win solution.
6. Attempting to persuade all individuals involved in a decision with a single solution is like a politician expecting to please all of the people all of the time.

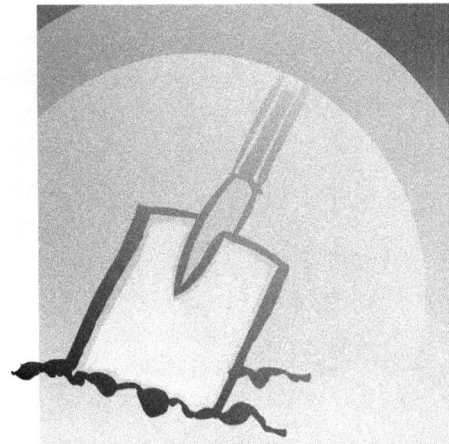

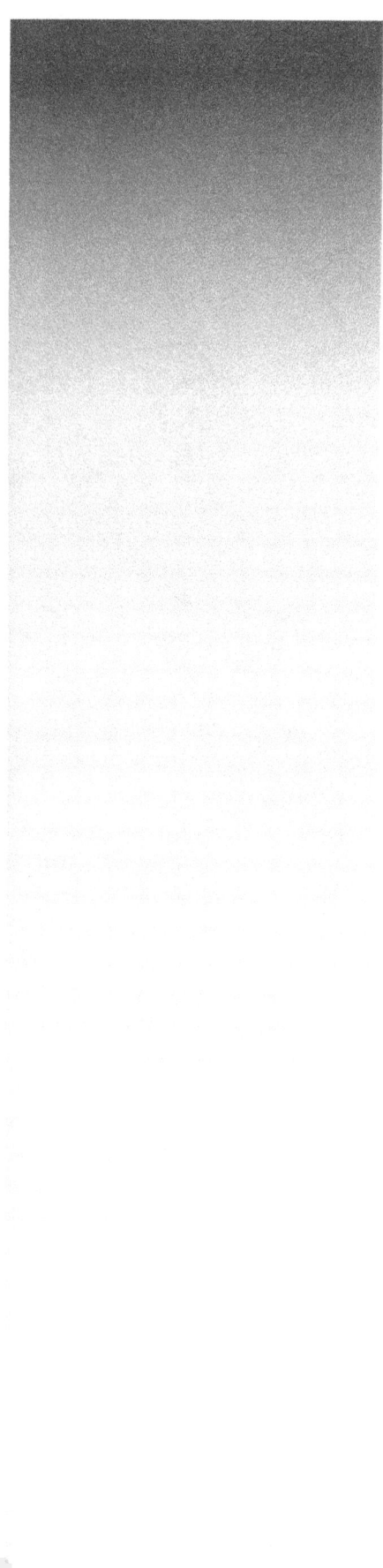

Chapter 7   Planning = Confidence

CHAPTER SNAPSHOT
• Minimizing the risk of failure by planning, Negative Planning and adjusting the resource team's expectations
• Building the team's confidence leads to trust-based relationships, which can ultimately lead to a strong referral network

Each aspect of RDS should be linked to style assessments, resource balancing and planning, all in an effort to minimize the risk of failing. Customer behavioral styles (DISC), job responsibilities, goals, measurements, work experiences and preconceived opinions make each customer a collection of separate and unique individuals. A blended resource team needs a well-planned strategy that should include a list of questions for them to ask as well as answers to the questions they may be asked. Accompanying a salesperson or manager to resolve a specific customer problem face-to-face can be stressful for some non-sales resources, but it is tolerable for most. However, many accountants, lawyers, billing coordinators and design engineers who are expected to plan, rehearse, execute and follow up on a prospective customer "cold call" will tell you they will avoid or procrastinate because they are simply not comfortable performing that task. What is the underlying cause for the lack of desire to make a sales

> *What is the underlying cause for the lack of desire to make a sales call? Confidence.*

> *It doesn't take magic to earn the trust of a prospective or current customer, but it does require solid planning.*

call? Confidence. In this chapter we explore how an initial burst of confidence in non-salespeople can help them more comfortably communicate directly with current and prospective customers.

I imagine any magician would say the easiest way for them to overcome fear when performing a risky magic trick is to simply remove the risk. Whenever I watch the "Greatest Magic Tricks Revealed" television specials, I get annoyed at how simple it really is for the magician to produce the illusion. To us, Harry Houdini defied death every day, but to him, there was little risk because of his pre-illusion planning. Houdini's plan was usually to hide the key to his handcuffs or exploit his double-jointed physical manipulation in order to squeeze out of the ropes and other precarious situations. His planning allowed him to break free from whatever apparatus he was attached to or locked into at the bottom of a tank of water. Houdini didn't perform any real magic and was seldom ever really at risk. However, he did plan, practice and master some unique God-given physical skills and strengths to create the illusion of performing magic and risking his life, thus entertaining people all over the world.

It doesn't take magic to earn the trust of a prospective or current customer, but it does require solid planning. Initial conversations with a prospect can be froth with risk, from not knowing how to start or what to say, to how to respond to questions or comments from the prospect. The unknown can inevitably lead to the risk of having to suffer through a mortifying and miserable failure. The possibility of rejection can terrify most non-salespeople, leaving them without the confidence or courage to proceed. When designing RDS, not only did we examine why many people failed and/or feared failing when attempting to establish new buyer relationships, but we also looked at what could be done to minimize the risk of failure in order to maximize the confidence and courage needed to proceed and succeed. Non-salespeople will more consistently initiate new customer relationships if, like the great magicians, they know that their risk of failure is significantly reduced or removed. Removing the risk of failure can be accomplished in two ways.

First, help the non-sales resources get comfortable dealing with customers by changing the assumed rules of prospecting. Plan for and encourage the team to change their own expectations and the generally accepted definition of prospecting so that 100% of the risk and chance of failing is removed. Think of it as Houdini carrying a second hidden key, just in case the first one didn't work as planned. Planning a customer interaction and changing expectations is the back up key to removing the risk of failure. Prospecting historically has been defined as

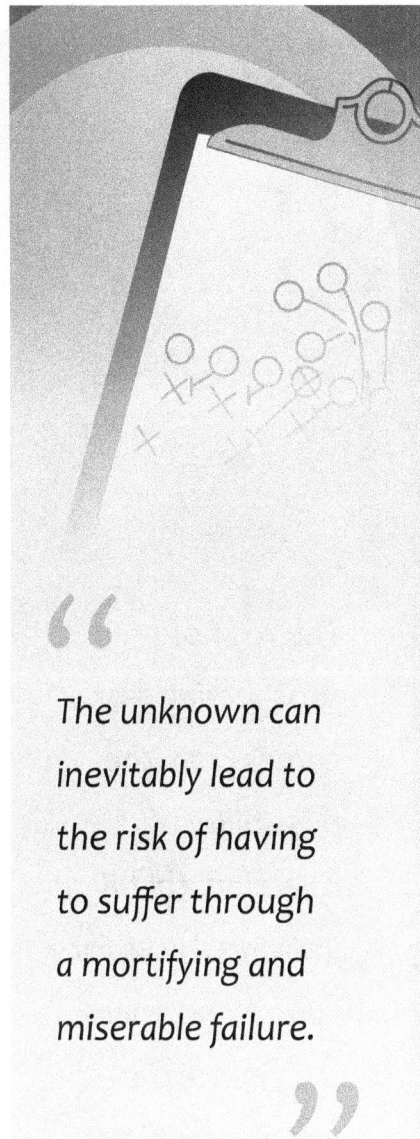

The unknown can inevitably lead to the risk of having to suffer through a mortifying and miserable failure.

> *The root of prospecting fear comes from the possibility of rejection, that if an individual asks for something, there is a chance the answer could be "No."*

discovering or developing a potential customer by asking for an appointment or an invitation to make a presentation or provide a price quote. The root of prospecting fear comes from the possibility of rejection, that if an individual asks for something, there is a chance that the answer could be "No." However, if a non-sales resource plans to not ask for anything, he or she cannot be told "no." To increase the odds of not losing, the control shifts and the resource is the one in the position to say no by disqualifying or eliminating the prospective customer instead of attempting to create customer interest. When the expectation is turned upside down, the confidence of a non-sales resource increases sharply. If the goal of prospecting is to quickly eliminate uninterested customers instead of the more common approach of attempting to generate interest, then success is measured by disqualifying uninterested customers or getting to "No" fast. This approach saves valuable resource time which can be invested elsewhere and in other prospective customers who do show a need or interest. Disqualifying makes getting to "no, I don't have any needs" the goal.

Another way to minimize the risk of failure is to lessen the fear of the unknown and unexpected. Once again, we examined not only why most people fear initiating new relationships, but also what needs to be done to address the root cause of that fear. If an individual plans for as many possible customer objections as possible, they can feel better prepared and therefore, less afraid. Utilizing the first Core Element, Negative Planning for Positive Results, resources are better prepared for almost anything anyone can throw at them. Planning for the unpleasant, often unexpected issues prospective customers introduce generally translates into a more confident attitude. That confident attitude can propel non-salespeople into discussions with prospective customers. Negative Planning from a customer's viewpoint should take into account each individual behavioral style (DISC), job responsibility, measurements and pressures as well as other possible influences each individual could be experiencing.

Many see potential in this approach but quickly dismiss it as being impractical. I disagree, because I personally learned to reduce my fear of failure by being better prepared. Like most people, I've managed to avoid many of the things that either scared me or I didn't like. Speaking to large groups was something I simply could not avoid, especially when it became a part of my job. Looking back, I never really minded talking in front of people until an unexpected triggering event completely dissolved my self-confidence. I was scheduled to make a presentation to the Board of Directors for Bethlehem Steel the week after my mother died in a car accident. Perhaps I was still in a state of shock, but the minute I got up to speak, my legs felt like rubber and it was all I could do to keep from falling to the floor.

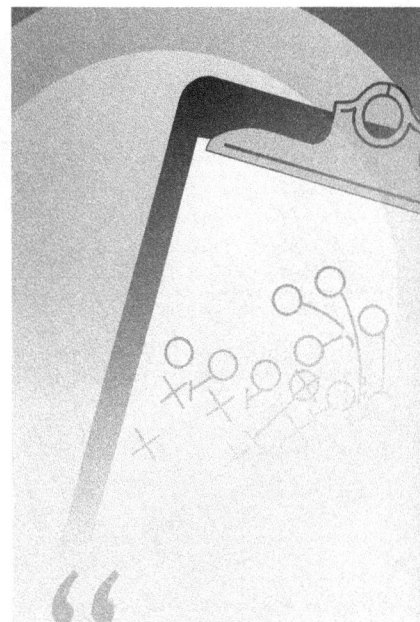

Planning for the unpleasant, often unexpected issues prospective customers introduce generally translates into a more confident attitude.

Although I managed to survive that day without fainting, every time I had to speak to any group, even small groups I experienced as Mel Brooks would say, "High Anxiety." Because my livelihood depended on speaking to small and large groups, I had to quickly learn to overcome the fear a public presentation could create. That took Negative Planning, anticipating the worst that could happen and having several well-planned options just in case the worst thing imaginable actually happened. In other words, I had to slowly dissolve my fear of public speaking by intentionally anticipating and planning around my greatest fears by being better prepared.

A flashback to my freshman year in high school provides the inspiration for my next, perhaps more entertaining example. As a teenager, I actually witnessed someone else who developed the ability to overcome a paralyzing fear. I'm not talking about the fashion statements most of us look back to the 1970s and shake with fear; the long hair, bell-bottom pants and polyester sports coats. I'm referring to a skinny, redheaded little dweeb named George O'Reilly, who experienced perhaps the worst moment of his life and the most unimaginable incident a freshman boy could encounter. Coach Russo was our cantankerous 65 year-old gym teacher, who decades before smoking bans, actually sat in his chair and chain-smoked cigarettes inside the gymnasium while we exercised. He would say, "Gentleman,

I'm what is called a piece of work!" He was definitely a piece of something when it came to preparing us for the President's Physical Fitness Program. Each day we were required to do as many as one hundred push-ups and sit-ups, or at least try to. I remember the sit-ups because I had to hold Dennis Fumei's ankles on the floor while he grunted and farted his way to 100 and both of us cursed his mother's potato salad. The rope climb was another element in the President's program. Nearly everyday, Coach Russo verbally trodden George O'Reilly in front of the entire class in an effort to motivate him to climb the rope that hung from the ceiling of the gym. George refused every request to climb. However, one day following a direct order from Coach Russo and despite his secret fear of heights, George ascended up the rope and reached the half way point before making the mistake of looking down. George froze in fear when he realized he was fifteen feet off the ground. He just hung there; he wouldn't go up or come down so all we could do was gather around and encourage George to try to come down the same way he went up. Growing impatient, Coach Russo began yelling even more, causing George to hang on tighter and cry harder.

After reflecting on his limited options, George did the most unexpected thing; he managed to climb off the rope and onto the top of the retracted basketball backboard. This appeared to be a poorly conceived follow-up plan

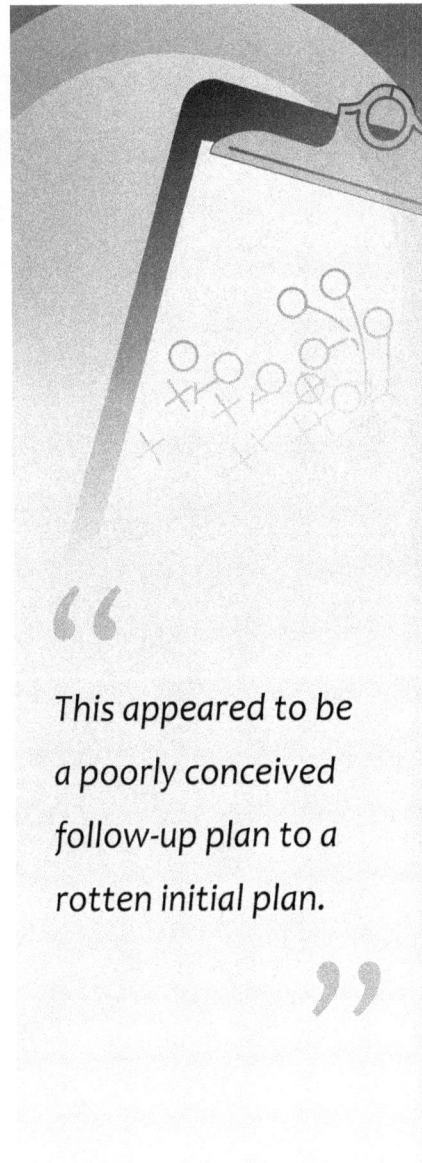

> *This appeared to be a poorly conceived follow-up plan to a rotten initial plan.*

to a rotten initial plan. However, there George O'Reilly stood, atop the retracted basketball backboard, fifteen feet above the crowd. He was clinging to the steel supports and profusely refusing to move amid a barrage inspirational suggestions that only Coach Russo was capable of hurling while his cigarette dangled from his lower lip. I've often wondered if George felt the way he looked, like a circus clown looking down from the high wire at the crowd of spectators below, half praying that he'd fall and the other half just enjoying the greatest spectacle on earth. Most of us were convinced that George would have set up a residence on that backboard if it hadn't been for Arnold Kellshaw, our kind Gomer Pile look-a-like janitor. Arnold rolled a large ladder out of a nearby storage closet, climbed it and carried George back to the floor. Had that been the end of the story, it would have no place in this book because it wouldn't do a thing to convince people to negative plan and overcome their fears.

About six years after George O'Reilly made his way back to terra firma in the gymnasium, he somehow mustered the courage to take up skydiving. Yes, skydiving. I was watching the evening news one night in the late 1970's when I saw a guy parachute off of one of the World Trade Center towers. The newscaster reported the mystery jumper as escaping into traffic, most likely whisked away by a waiting car. I recall my father saying, "Look at that crazy bastard!"

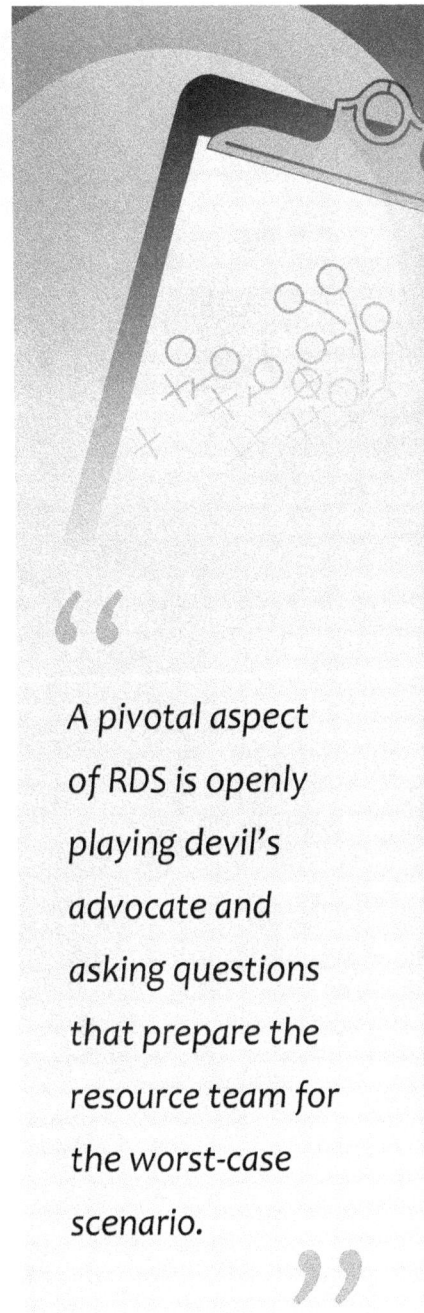

and when I did, I realized it was George. All I could think was how and why the hell did George O'Reilly overcome his fear of heights and jump off the World Trade Center to prove it? It would take me several months before learning the answer.

To some non-salespeople, the fear of selling is as daunting as climbing the rope or jumping off a 110-story building. However, preparing for the climb, jump or sales call with a step-by-step plan will build confidence and skills, especially while Negative Planning for what might go wrong. A pivotal aspect of RDS is openly playing devil's advocate and asking questions that prepare the resource team for the worst-case scenario. In George's case, his worst-case outcomes were either dying from the jump, or living and getting arrested. Every question for a customer interaction is planned and tailored based on behavioral style (DISC) and job responsibility for both the resources asking the questions and the individual prospect being asked. Additionally, a list of questions that the prospect may ask is also brainstormed with the worst possible questions (and answers) listed first. Resources are rehearsed on how to answer the tough questions, which minimizes the "deer in the headlights" look of fear.

Before making the first phone call or face-to-face customer visit, the resource team is assembled and balanced

> *A pivotal aspect of RDS is openly playing devil's advocate and asking questions that prepare the resource team for the worst-case scenario.*

according to DISC style. The team then determines individual responsibilities and a call plan, complete with objectives and questions to ask and be asked. Although most possible scenarios are explored, no one can plan for or anticipate everything. However, nearly every time our resource team approaches the prospect, they have a greater degree of confidence and less anxiety because they are better prepared than the time before. Resources usually say the customer visit went extremely well and that they were ready for nearly everything that came up, including the nasty issues they were well prepared to handle. Our resources enjoy the credibility and confidence they portray to prospects, and most not only have fun on customer visits but also volunteer to participate in future visits!

Professionally, the most extreme example I've experienced is that of an individual who made a 180 degree change and now loves visiting customers. Janet is an operationally brilliant plant manager whose introverted nature and paralyzing fear of failing prevented her from visiting face to face with customers for over five years. However, within one week of participating in a RDS planning session that provided her with questions and strategies, she found the courage not only to make her first customer visit in years, she actually enjoyed it. She went on to lead countless customer visits and to this day looks forward to the interaction with prospective customers. Her colleagues commented on her transformation and Janet credited the change to the confidence she received from planning the actual questions to ask and be asked.

Planning, expecting the worst and gaining confidence can make a skyscraper of a prospective customer visit seem like just another casual conversation between two old high school friends. To me, team Negative Planning for customer interactions is like the day I was asked to be one of three get-a-way drivers that George planned for when he jumped out of a small airplane over a state psychiatric hospital. I was nervous, but felt confident I could quickly disappear down a number of the country roads I had carefully mapped out in advance should George land near my car and the police choose to chase us. Three months after George's triumphant jump from the World Trade Center, George O'Reilly gathered his parachute and stuffed it into the back of my parent's station wagon and we raced down a small country road, away from the state psychiatric hospital. As planned, the police pursued the other two decoy cars and we raced along unchallenged. At that moment, I realized that George had overcome his fear of failing. We both unknowingly did our share of Negative Planning to the point where we simply could not fail because we were better rehearsed, had more options and therefore the adrenalin-pumped confidence that convinced us that the fear of failure was simply not going to get in the way of executing a successful plan.

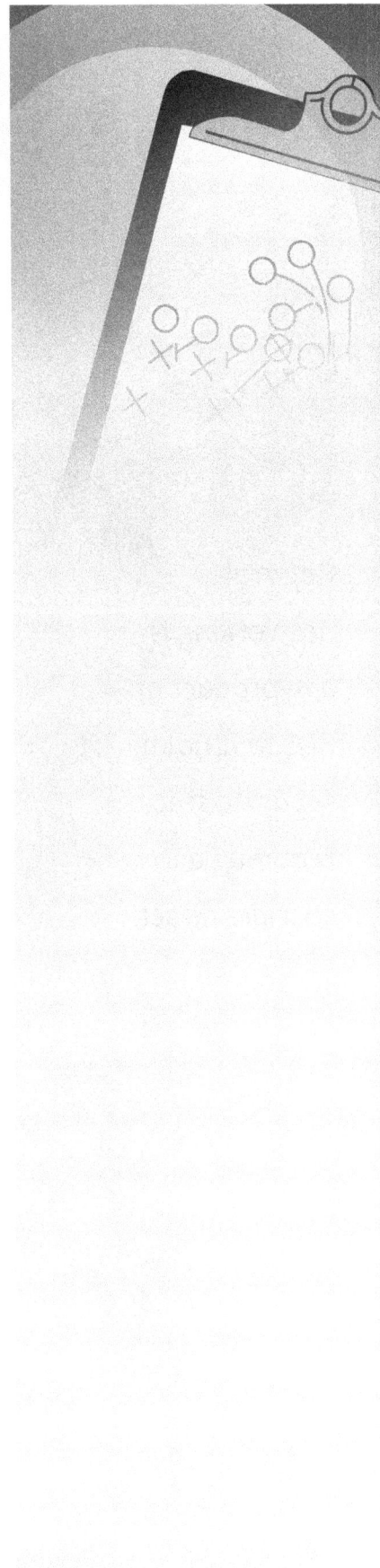

"

Referral
networking is
a byproduct of
RDS, but not a
separate step
requiring a
special skill set.

"

In a book about selling, planning and prospecting, many of you may be wondering why we haven't put a great deal of emphasis on the topic of networking. Networking is indeed a critical component for securing new clients in almost every business. Unfortunately, many view networking as passing out and collecting contact information at trade shows and chamber luncheons, then following up with cold call style phone calls or face-to-face meetings. Those skilled at networking have obtained those skills from years of experience conversing with people. Generally speaking, non-sales, middle and low-level resources are not experienced at networking, however RDS provides the added benefit of value-based referral networking when no skilled networking professionals are available. Referral networking is a byproduct of RDS, but not a separate step requiring a special skill set. It is important to understand that like prospecting, not all resources are comfortable with the task of networking and therefore only those with the confidence to network provide that benefit to the team.

Successful referral networking is developing genuine interest in an individual's personal and/or professional life and fostering a relationship based on that interest. Genuine, not contrived interest leads to valuable relationships that generate trust and loyalty. Non-sales resources have a natural propensity to help others, seldom asking for or expecting anything in return. That is how RDS referral networks are built. Referrals and opportunities for more referrals are the result of the value and assistance current customers see in the resource team, not the other way around. Some salespeople see network contacts as a source for selling and that transparency can dissuade a potential customer. In the day-to-day course of servicing current customers, RDS resources gain confidence through helping and partnering with current and prospective customers with the solutions and answers they provide, not by selling. RDS participants find that resource teams on both sides of the relationship tend to freely talk up their positive associations with others and that networking byproduct leads to curious new referrals.

Similar to RDS's qualifying and disqualifying prospective customers, RDS does not use networking as a method to promote or sell anything. Genuine interest in an individual should spark value-based follow-up where both parties genuinely want to help the other. Trusted and loyal contacts tend to promote the individuals and companies they trust. The more exposure and assistance an individual or business provides, the greater the probability a potential client will trust. It is at that moment a potential client becomes curious enough to develop a relationship that eventually spawns referrals and other networking opportunities. Referral networking is the direct result of planning, Negative Planning and the confidence non-sales resources gain from the RDS methodology.

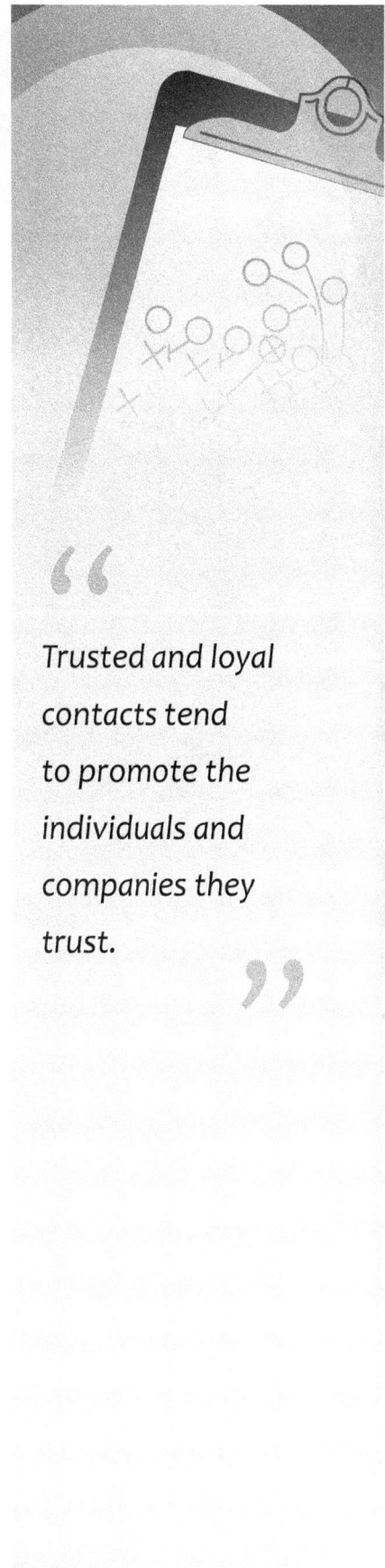

> *Trusted and loyal contacts tend to promote the individuals and companies they trust.*

Chapter 7 Highlights

1. Reduce the risk of failure to increase the odds of success.
2. Change the rules and definition of prospecting by measuring success with getting to "No."
3. Plan and Negative Plan for Positive Results to lessen paralysis caused by fear of failure.
4. Retention-fed growth can ideally minimize the need for prospecting. Referral networking is a byproduct of RDS. If RDS is properly executed, satisfied customers may refer the resource team to other companies in search of highly trusted problem solving partners.

Chapter 8   What Do You Know?

CHAPTER SNAPSHOT
- Knowing more about the prospect from the prospect's viewpoint offers a blended resource team a significant competitive advantage
- Challenging resource teams to critically assess what they know about the customer in order to seek out in the missing data

Removing risk and Negative Planning can make jumping out of airplanes and conducting confident cold calls a possibility. But the first step in preparing for a customer call or meeting actually starts with a simple resource team brainstorming exercise, the foundational building block of planning and making a cold call or customer visit. Team brainstorming is another important part of the confidence building process because the answers to questions the resources ask themselves are fact-based. When a resource team plans and properly anticipates customer needs and objections based on what is known for a fact, building knowledge becomes more of a focus than selling a customer. This approach is designed to separate what the team knows to be an irrefutable fact from what is opinion, hearsay or a flat out guess. It also reveals the missing pieces that need to be uncovered or reasonably ascertained by logically connecting the facts with opinions and assumptions. Once the information is collected and realistically assessed, the team can begin putting together

possible scenarios from which to build a plan.

The collection of data is based on an exercise we call "Knowledge Quest," and when combined with brainstorming, becomes the sixth Core Element. This entire thought process came as a direct result of my sitting in an airplane on a tarmac for several hours with nothing to do. I was still fuming over my most recent discussion with my sales team over reducing prices. It was the late 1990's and I was the General Manager of a state-of-the-art processing and distribution start-up in the midwest. The company I worked for spared no expense in building, staffing and filling our new facility with the best available equipment and resources. Our target was the agricultural equipment market, which was notorious for very high quality standards. Our competitors, although more established in the marketplace, simply could not compete with the surface quality and specification tolerances we knew our new facility could routinely deliver. Despite what I perceived to be a significant competitive advantage, our salespeople could not secure a trial order or any order unless I agreed to meet the latest in a long line of decreasing price points. I surmised that my sales team could not be asking the right questions and therefore did not know their customers or their own product advantages as well as I thought they should. As I sat on the tarmac, I started to write a list of questions that any decent salesperson should know about their customers.

Three hours and 200 questions later, the pilot announced that we were next for takeoff. The questions became the starting point of the inaugural "Knowledge Quest" game, prepared to ambush an unsuspecting sales team and stop unsubstantiated requests to lower price and margin.

When I returned home from my trip, one by one, each of our five sales and service teams entered the conference room to play Knowledge Quest. The rules were to simply pick one customer that the team knew best and answer questions that most salespeople would consider common. I labeled three flip charts "We Know," "We Think We Know" and "We Don't Know," then started asking questions, some of which are included in the following box. When they claimed to know things they only thought they knew, I challenged them to honestly assess and properly categorize their answers as "We Think We Know" or "We Don't Know."

The following pages contain a sample of some of the 200 questions I asked my sales team that day.

CORE ELEMENT 6

Implement Knowledge Quest and Brainstorming

Concentrate on learning as many facts as possible about the customer and their decision process. Challenge the resource team by categorizing "We Know," "We Think We Know," and "We Don't Know" to differentiate the company. Knowledge Quest brainstorming is a self-teaching challenge that builds confidence and inspires individuals and teams to learn what customers need by questioning and listening.

Knowledge Quest - Sample Questions

1. What does this client produce or what do they do to generate revenue? (Do you know that for a fact? How do you know that as a fact?)
2. Does this client/prospect fit the criteria of our niche?
3. Does this client have a "compelling event" that would trigger the need for our product quality, tolerances or delivery standards?
   a. What is that event?
   b. Do all the decision makers understand that they have this need?
   c. How do you know?
   d. Have you asked every decision maker?
4. Who are the decision makers?
5. Do you know for a fact, and do you have a complete list of all decision makers, influencers, approvers, potential blockers and users of our products and services?
6. What is the decision-making process?
7. Is there one or a few decision makers driving the decision-making process or does there need to be a consensus?
   a. How do you know that?
8. Is there a decision maker who is not on board with the company's current course of action?
9. Is that person influential enough to blackball or completely derail this process at some future point?
10. Who actually makes the decision at our company to source the

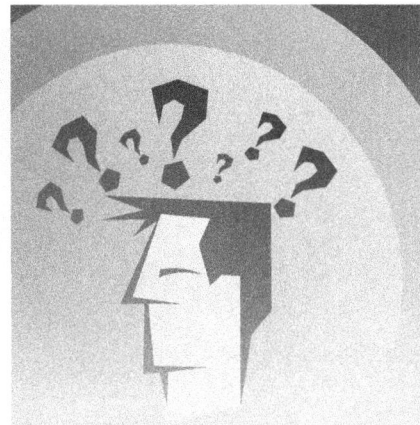

products and services we purchase?
   a. Is it one person or several?
   b. Do you know that for a fact?
11. If you don't know all those who impact our decision to purchase, how can you be so certain you know everyone involved in purchasing for your customer?
12. Would you feel comfortable helping the purchasing agent arrive at our quantifiable value primarily through questioning (not telling or explaining)?
   a. What about the CFO and finance people?
   b. What about the operations people?
13. What is the client's image of our industry? (Positive or negative? Why?)
14. What is the client's image of us?
   a. Does each decision maker share that opinion?
   b. Do you know that to be a fact? How?
15. Are you comfortable reading and adapting to each decision maker's style, needs and personality?
16. Are you successful?
   a. How do you know for a fact?
17. What is the behavioral style of each individual involved in the decision-making process?
18. What is this company's annual sales in dollars?
19. Are their sales trending up or down?
20. In what stage does the company see itself — Emerging, Rapid

> *My team was astonished how little they really knew about their customers.*

Growth, a Market Leader or Sustained Market Leader?
21. Who are their competitors?
22. What are the key performance indicators the client monitors?
23. Why are these important to them? Have you asked them?
24. What are the key risks your client sees for the coming 12 months?
    a. 36 months?
25. What could the possible impact be on the business and executives?
26. (If your client has multiple locations) What percentage of their total cost and profit do they currently receive from each location?
27. How are the executives of the company compensated?
28. Does the executive group share in the savings you generate for them?
29. What drives their behavior?
    a. Do you know this for a fact?

When I had asked the 200th question, we tallied up the answers on the flip charts. Overall, less than 5% of the answers fell into "I Know." Considering this game was played based on the customers the teams knew best, this was not a fun game for anyone. My team was astonished how little they really knew about their customers. Then, with a vengeful and crushing flashback to the three hot hours I spent on the tarmac, I concluded with a harmless "Just a few last questions."

30. What do you really know about your customers, competitors and your own company?
31. Do you know enough about your customer, competition and company to provide facts to support your recommendation to reduce price or give away a service?
32. How do you think your competition would fare if given this same challenge?

My very last question, "Would you like to do this exercise for all of the customers that you are responsible for?" got a resounding, "We know for a fact the answer to that question is No!" I guess they learned a valuable lesson!

What Knowledge Quest demonstrates is that the resource team does not have to know the answers to all of the questions, because as soon as a question is asked, circumstances and people change, making it impossible to keep up. However, the thirst to ask questions and better understand customers needs from their point of view differentiates the resource team from the competition.

Years after piloting Knowledge Quest on my unsuspecting sales team, Chris and I generated several thousand custom tailored questions based on industry to help our clients know their clients better than anyone else. Assuming that the competition was either as smart as or

> *However, the thirst to ask questions and better understand customers needs from their point of view differentiates the resource team from the competition.*

> *The questions I asked of the team became the very questions they not only remembered, but sought answers to.*

as incompetent as we were, and if we only knew 5% of the answers, we assumed our competitor also knew 5%. For us to constantly push our team to know just 1% more, 6% of the questions equates to knowing 20% more than the competition, possibly giving us an advantage at least in fact-based knowledge. How many answers are needed to differentiate? How many questions get us to 1%? Out of the 200 I used, knowing the answers to only two more questions could make a difference. Adding questions from the Knowledge Quest to a lunch meeting or at the end of a formal business meeting builds on the team's knowledge, provides a way to keep up on the ever-changing answers and allows for a solid, fact-based differentiation. In true RDS, there are multiple resources communicating with various players in the decision-making process. Therefore it is not only possible, it is likely that a resource team consisting of five or 10 members could ask dozens of additional questions at any given time, thus providing a significant differentiation and advantage over the competition.

The most significant benefit of this exercise was that my team although embarrassed at first, never approached me again with price concessions that weren't based in fact. For them, Knowledge Quest evolved into a continuous self-teaching effort. The questions I asked of the team became the very questions they not only remembered, but sought answers to. The next time they communicated with a customer and every time thereafter, my team became better prepared and much more knowledgeable about their company, competitors and their customers.

Our volume grew, our prices stabilized and actually began to increase, but more importantly, our sales force earned the reputation of being more professional and better prepared than the rest of the industry. Our sales team proficiency mirrored our state-of-the-art process facility and we were branded, "The Dream Team."

RDS takes an overall view of what we discovered in Knowledge Quest and includes it in the brainstorming segment. We take our prioritized pipeline, select one target prospect at a time and start to list everything we know about them. Interestingly, as learned in Knowledge Quest, most of what gets captured starts in the "We Think We Know" category. When challenged, some of these responses are moved to "We Don't Know," but very little gets listed under "We Know." A very sobering lesson learned from this exercise is that for the vast majority of us, decisions are made based on assumptions. Those initial assumptions are merely bastardized facts that we stack even more assumptions on, and then we use that pile of garbage as the foundation for making even more decisions. As I sat on that tarmac, I realized my frustration came from approving price reductions for countless customers simply

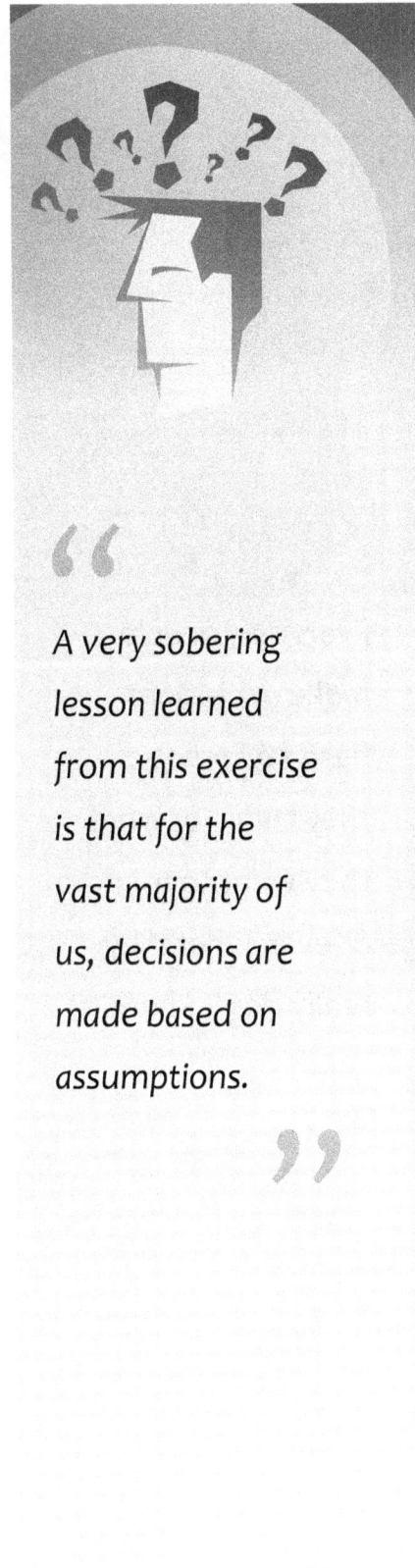

> *A very sobering lesson learned from this exercise is that for the vast majority of us, decisions are made based on assumptions.*

> *Everyday, people make decisisions based on what they think, or what they want to think or even what they really don't know.*

because the salesperson "thought" he lost an order due to price. My uninformed decision to cut the price had lead to another equally uninformed, but much more ignorant decision to beat my own price the next day if an order still had not been received.

Is it any wonder why ill-conceived assumptions fuel the paltry cold call success rate of less than 3%? Everyday, people make decisions based on what they think, or what they want to think or even what they really don't know. Seldom do we take the time to truly drill down and understand the facts before making assumptions, recommendations and decisions.

In a RDS brainstorming session, participants challenge the information collected and the category placed in (We Know, We Think We Know, We Don't Know) until there is a solid understanding of what still needs to be learned about the customer. If there is truly a place to utilize Negative Planning, this is it. Criticize, question and challenge your own data until you are confident the team is viewing the strategy, data and questions from the customer's viewpoint, not your own . Although this process sounds frustrating, it is a very effective way to give the non-sales resource team a fighting chance, dealing with facts and becoming a more trustworthy supplier. The ultimate result of Knowledge Quest is not what is known or not known, but learning and better understanding where the team needs to go to fill in the missing information, providing a clear direction and a plan. The fact-based Negative Planning contained in RDS can increase non-sales resource confidence and in turn, their prospect-to-closed-customer success rate, depending on the disqualifying and planning circumstances.

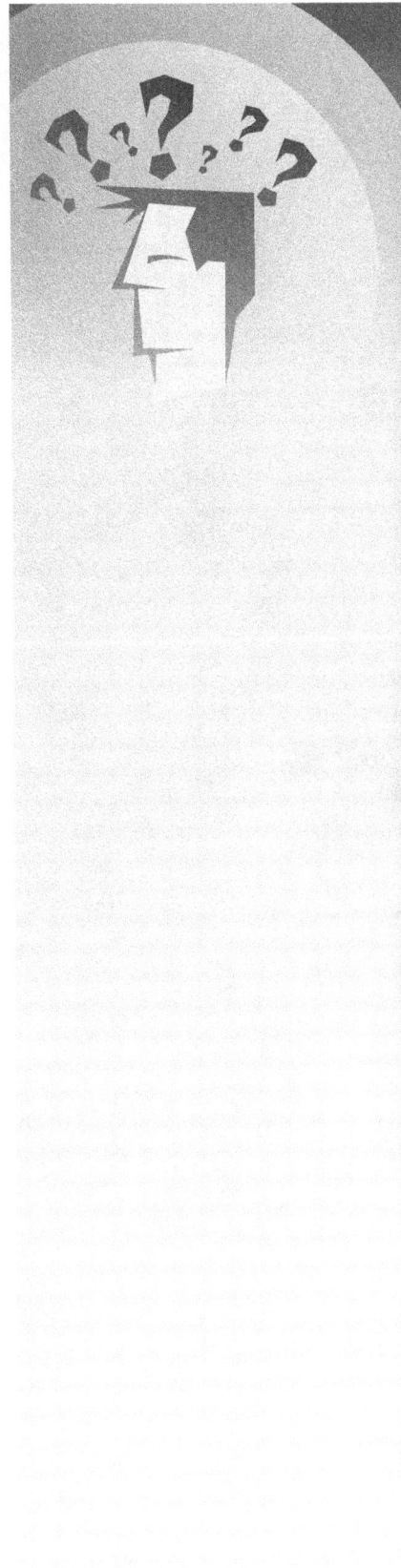

Chapter 8 Highlights

1. RDS is fact-based. A team of resources with a question-focus can learn more from the customer's viewpoint than a single individual because they can ask more questions of more people and therefore collect more information.

2. The sixth Core Element, *Implement Knowledge Quest and Brainstorming*, is designed to uncover as many facts as possible about:

   a. The customer (the company and the individuals)

   b. Your competition

   c. The customer's competition

   d. Your organization and its true value in the customer's eyes

3. Knowledge Quest can increase "We Know" while reducing "We Don't Know" because team members challenge each other and ultimately connect logical assumptions with facts, thus identifying the informational gaps that still need to be filled.

4. Challenge yourself and your team by properly categorizing "We Know," "We Think We Know" and "We Don't Know." This will differentiate your organization and make your resource team more effective and valuable, a significant competitive advantage.

5. Knowledge is power, with power being the ability to confidently communicate from the customer's viewpoint. Develop questions you should ask as well as those you could be asked by the customer. Challenge yourself. We've developed several hundred questions in each category for various industries. You should attempt to do the same.

6. Once deployed, this self-teaching challenge inspires individuals and teams to utilize questioning and listening to foster better decisions and communication habits.

Chapter 9 Stages of Buying

CHAPTER SNAPSHOT
• Understanding that buyers buy, sellers do not sell
• Objectively reviewing the customer's options and finding the best overall solution by assisting buyers with connecting the dots can be more successful that old-style selling approaches

As the game changes from selling to buying, the rules of the game must change as well. Historically, salespeople consciously or subconsciously walked through a sales cycle. A typical sales cycle consists of a seller identifying a prospect's needs, then presenting a price or proposal for a product or service, and hopefully negotiating and closing an agreement with the customer. Some salespeople shortened this cycle to the ABC's of selling, "Always Be Closing." Cheesy and downright ineffective, the shortcut gave old-style salespeople an even worse reputation for asking for the order until they got it. Although some traditional salespeople still practice and believe in some type of sales cycle, approaching the buyer solely from the seller's viewpoint can disregard the Buyer's Stages of Buying.

Unfortunately, many companies continue to train new salespeople with philosophies rooted in the 1950's. To ensure that the salespeople follow these sales process steps, some companies "certify" their salespeople. One example is

> *Unfortunately, many companies continue to train new salespeople with philosophies rooted in the 1950's.*

CORE ELEMENT 7

The Buyer's Stages of Buying

Evaluate Current Level of Satisfaction

⬇

Realize a Need

⬇

Review Options

⬇

Sourcing Decision and Implementation

⬇

Satisfaction After Delivery

RDS has no sales cycle because everything in RDS is measured and guided by the buyer's decision-making process. Start by focusing on the customer's level of satisfaction and end with sustaining the customer's level of satisfaction.

a Fortune 500 corporation my wife worked for several years ago. The sales training program consisted of a three-day session followed by a certification, then another two days of follow-up training. After the first session, my wife asked if I would help her role play a 20-step selling process so she could pass her certification. At first I was shocked at any sales process with 20 steps, then I laughed at Step 1 of their sales call procedure: "Firm handshake, look the customer in the eye and give a warm greeting." Other seemingly simple steps followed, but it was the 7th or 8th step that sent me over the edge, reiterating the customer's needs with, "That's what you want, isn't it?" I refused to help her role play anymore. She did pass the certification, but also told with me that other "certified" company executives consistently apologized after joint sales calls when they took the lead, saying they did a terrible job of following their process steps even though they secured the customer utilizing their own strengths! In follow-up training, my wife's training manager made a statement to the class of 100 plus participants that they were going "back to the basics." All of the company's customer-facing employees would be retrained at a cost of several million dollars because after three years, they found no one was really following the cumbersome sales process. This is a textbook case of malicious obedience, when an individual is told to do something they know will not work, follows instructions knowing it will fail, and in the end damages the reputation

and efforts of the misguided idiot or idiots who made them do it in the first place. My wife admitted most employees passed their certification only to revert back to what they were comfortable with. I wonder how many corporations spend money on sales training that in the end has no impact on employees, customers and ultimately the bottom line?

If you believe that well-informed consumers buy, and therefore don't want to be sold, then the seller's view of the current buying process needs to mirror the buyer's viewpoint. The most fundamental concept of RDS is to view everything through the customers' eyes. With that comes the end of a sales cycle for a seller and advent of sellers focusing primarily on the Buyers's Stages of Buying, the seventh Core Element, which is fundamentally different from the seller's sales cycle. Buyers generally begin by evaluating their current level of satisfaction and if they realize they have a need, may review options, then make and implement a sourcing decision. Once the buyer takes delivery of the solution, the buyer once again can evaluate satisfaction, starting the sequence over again.

Evaluate Current Level of Satisfaction

In the first stage, a buyer evaluates their current level of satisfaction. This stage has nothing to do with a seller identifying a buyer's needs. In fact, it has absolutely nothing to do with selling and only involves the potential buyer. If

> " The most fundamental concept of RDS is to view everything through the customer's eyes. "

> *Only when the buyer is less than completely satisfied with their current situation can the second stage, realizing there is a need, happen.*

a potential buyer is satisfied with their current situation, product, service and/or supplier, they are not even a buyer, at least not yet. If they are completely satisfied, nothing can be done to create a need for them to buy. Many salespeople passionately argue when we say a need cannot be created. It cannot! It can be revealed, but seldom created. For example, if someone is not satisfied with the car they own, attractive financing and dealer incentives might get their attention, inspire them to do some research and start the buying process, but only because there is a perceived need for a new car. However, if someone is content with their current car, will any incentive be a motivation to buy a new car? No, because there is no need for that person to buy a new car. The first stage of buying starts in the buyer's mind. Only when the buyer is less than completely satisfied with their current situation can the second stage, realizing that there is a need, happen.

So what should the resource team do if their prospect is completely satisfied, and therefore not currently categorized as a buyer? They should stay in touch with the prospective buyer, never sell or promote anything and focus only on building a relationship based on mutual trust. How is that accomplished? It is no different from what you do everyday with friends, family and coworkers. Genuinely express concern and empathy—offer opinions and suggestions when asked and help when possible. Never ask for

anything in return. This approach builds trust as well as an understanding of each other's personal and professional needs. If and when the buyer has a need, they will initiate their buying process, generally with someone they trust.

Realize a Need

The second stage of buying is the buyer's realization that they have a need. Some argue this is where selling begins, but it's not. The act of buying takes place when the buyer has a need and works with a trustworthy seller who can satisfy that need. Most old-style salespeople instinctively start to tell and sell when they discover a prospective customer with a need. That is why using RDS is counter-intuitive and not really about selling at all. Many old-style salespeople focus on generating a need by selling, promoting, pitching and closing—all activities that selfishly satisfy the old-style salesperson's allegiance to the seller's sales cycle. Unfortunately, the vast majority of sales failures occur because the salesperson does not capitalize on the only thing they can honestly influence - customer trust. Once again, does it come as any surprise that the average closing rate of prospective customers is less than 3%? Said another way, 97% of new customer prospecting ends in failure! Think of the wasted salaries, training, incentives, travel budgets and other costs—all to obtain a 97% failure rate!

> *Unfortunately, the vast majority of sales failures occur because the salesperson does not capitalize on the only thing they can honestly influence--customer trust.*

> *It becomes difficult for most people to resist the temptation of selling when a buyer's needs are obvious.*

RDS is counter-intuitive. It cautions the team not to sell and tell, which is exactly what most old-style salespeople do when they realize they have what a prospect needs. Think about what the average consumer does when they realize they need a new car or a new refrigerator. Most begin researching and evaluating possible options. Today, compliments of the Internet, the majority, if not all of the research and evaluation occur in the complete absence of a salesperson. But what triggered that research? A perceived need on the part of the buyer!

It becomes difficult for most people to resist the temptation of selling when a buyer's needs are obvious. What most old-style salespeople fail to understand and act on is the buyer's true need - a trustworthy person to help connect the dots and clearly evaluate all options, not just the option the seller is selling. Traditionally, connecting the dots was the equivalent of a salesperson pitching their solution with brochures and a long, memorized list of product features. In RDS, resources are encouraged to plan questions that are designed to quickly diagnose a buyer's needs and help a buyer connect the dots. The questions help reveal a buyer's issues and begin to uncover what impact those issues have on each individual involved in the buying process. Only then can a buyer and seller objectively evaluate the options available. Old-style salespeople dislike this approach because helping to connect the dots can risk

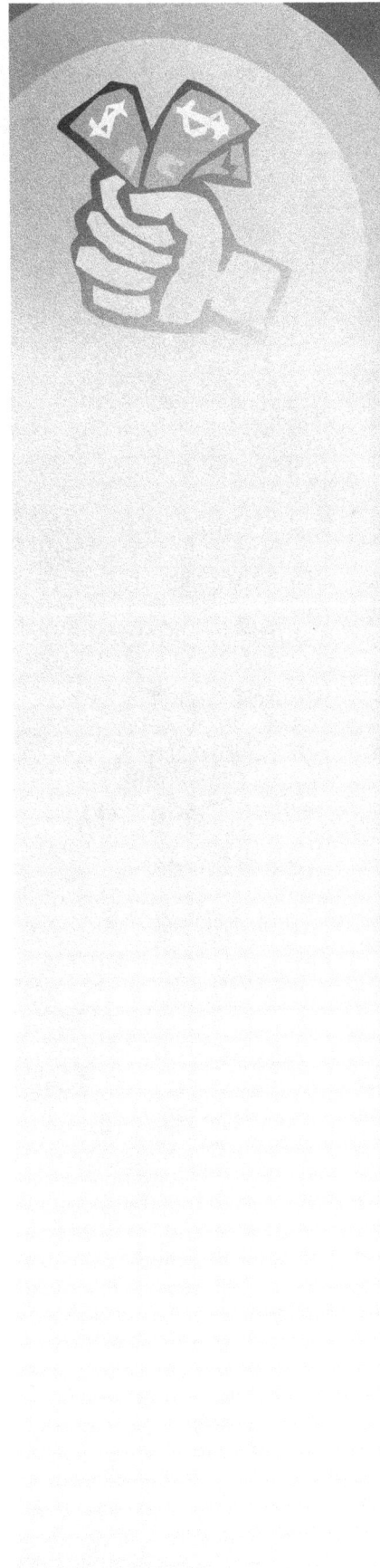

exposing a better option elsewhere, thwarting their attempt to sell their product or service. RDS would rather lose a customer and keep the trust than deceive a customer into choosing the seller's option, knowing it is not the best overall value for the buyer. Depending on the product or service, when a buyer is led astray from the best solution, trust in the seller can be irrevocably damaged, and if the buyer still decides to buy from the seller, they may change suppliers much sooner than anticipated. Sellers who assist a buyer in securing a more suitable option other than their own may feel they "lost," and that act will likely feel uncomfortable and counter-intuitive. However, doing the right thing from the buyer's viewpoint may mean that you'll never sell that buyer, but the sincere assistance should lead to referrals and a first-class reputation in the industry.

To help illustrate this point, several years ago, the managing partners of a very successful and growing regional services firm invited Chris and me to meet with their key people and provide options for training and facilitated coaching to help them expand their business development efforts. After several meetings, questions and evaluating their people and processes, it was apparent to us that they were very well situated with their clients and did not need our consulting or training. What they did appear to need was marketing communications expertise. Rather than attempt to sell them on training and coaching, although

> *Rarely does a seller's solution fit the buyer's need exactly without some type of adjustment, customization or negotiation.*

that's what they initially asked for, we recommended a small, but very skilled marketing specialist rather than sell something they didn't need. That decision to help them connect the dots with someone who could immediately address their issues started what has turned out to be a five year mutual referral relationship that has netted both companies significantly more that that original project would have generated.

Review Options

The third stage of buying, when a buyer reviews their options, the buyer and seller work together to mutually resolve concerns. Traditionally, this was referred to as the "bargaining" or "negotiating" stage of selling. Historically, resolution of each other's concerns was not either party's focus. Negotiations between buyer and seller do not need to be adversarial. Rarely does a seller's solution fit the buyer's need exactly without some type of adjustment, customization or negotiation. Mutual agreement and satisfaction, not just price, should be the goal of both sides. If a seller's number one priority is resolving a buyer's concerns, it becomes much easier to negotiate a win/win scenario for both parties. If a buyer understands that a seller requires a fair return and the seller appreciates his or her involvement in problem resolution, the trust-based relationship that started in the initial stage of the buying

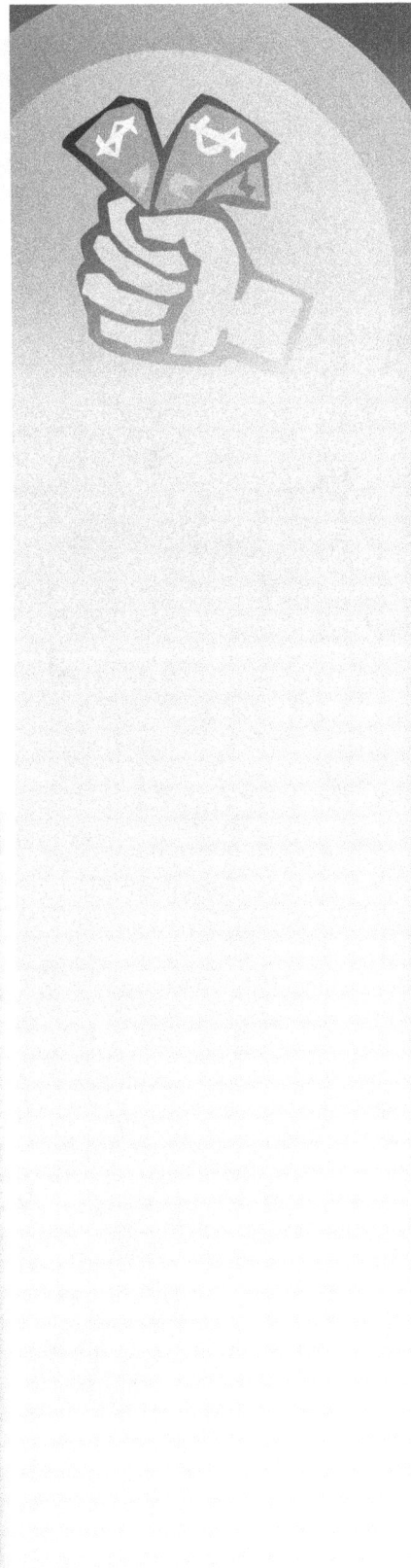

process grows stronger. Patience is key in this stage. As stated earlier, many old-style salespeople are quick to force a close, but time to build trust and uncover issues from the customer's viewpoint is not something that can be rushed. Rushing the process will inevitably lead to failure. Unfortunately, most selling styles often fail in this new paradigm because two of the three types of salespeople are doomed from the start.

Common Selling Styles

Selling for Sport: This irrational group approaches selling and negotiating as a sport and tries to win with the expectation that the customer will at least lose something. Where is the logic in winning at the risk of leaving a customer feeling that they lost?

The Giveaway Artist: This salesperson wants the customer to be so happy that the salesperson argues and negotiates harder within their own company than with their customer. In essence, they "give the store away." This lose/win scenario is just as irrational as the win/lose selling for sport but on the other end of the spectrum. This type of salesperson fails to see that loading up with ecstatic customers and an unhappy or unprofitable employer ultimately leads to disappointment for just about everyone involved.

The Ambassador: This group of sellers acknowledge that acquiring the customer's business must be reasonably profitable to the seller while providing a value to the customer. This style of win/win selling is not only a sound, long term strategy, but one of the cornerstones of RDS.

It's no surprise not all buyers are out to provide the seller with a win/win option. If a win/lose buyer is matched with a win/lose seller, the negotiating sport is intense, generated by each individual's selfish interests. If a lose/win seller is paired with a win/lose buyer, the buyer goes home with everything.

Sourcing Decision and Implementation

Many decisions are still made in a vacuum, where the seller has no influence on the buyer. RDS, if properly executed, disqualifies and selects buyers that will invite the resource team to participate in connecting the dots. RDS targets only prospects that genuinely want to partner. This may sound somewhat Pollyannaish to those who feel they have no choice but to deal with buyers who are out to secure a win/lose agreement every time. That may be the case depending on the type of commodity an individual or company provides. However, even the lowest commodity buyer has a decision-making process consisting of stakeholders who live and die based on product quality, delivery, value and service. RDS targets approvers, decision makers, influencers, recommenders, blockers and users, and establishes a quantifiable value for each. If a seller cannot realize a value, profit or benefit, why make the costly assumption that a marginal or unprofitable customer is better than no customer at all? RDS is still applicable in low margin business in severely competitive commodity markets, but it should not intentionally result in unprofitable business.

When a seller actively assists a buyer in formulating their decision with an objective review of the options, the ultimate decision should lead to a satisfied buyer. In RDS, when a buyer attempts to negotiate a win/lose agreement, they may win in the decision stage, but if the seller is taken advantage of, neither party will remain satisfied. Unhappy or unprofitable suppliers almost always reduce quality, delivery and service to compensate for low margins or to pay for what is sometimes referred to as the aggravation factor of dealing in a one-sided relationship. Therefore, in RDS it is important that the seller disqualify prospective customers who may want to buy, but who don't share the same win/win view of the buyer/seller relationship as the seller.

Satisfaction After Delivery

In traditional sales cycles, relationships between buyers and salespeople usually end at the close when some other customer service resource takes over for the salesperson that moves on to his next kill. Unlike a common sales cycle that begins with needs identification and ends with closing a customer, the Sourcing Decision and Implementation stage of the Buyer's Stages of Buying starts with a buyer's satisfaction (or lack thereof) and cycles back to the buyer's

If a seller cannot realize a value, profit or benefit, why make the costly assumption that a marginal or unprofitable customer is better than no customer at all?

satisfaction if it is done correctly. RDS doesn't end when the buyer decides to utilize the seller's solution because the resources involved in building the trust-based relationship that acquired the buyer are the same team who deliver and service the customer going forward. Assuming the Buyer's Stages of Buying were followed properly, if both parties ensured satisfaction on both sides, the two parties will remain partners until the customer becomes dissatisfied. If the trust is broken or a higher value solution becomes available, the dissatisfaction begins the Buyer's Stages of Buying all over again.

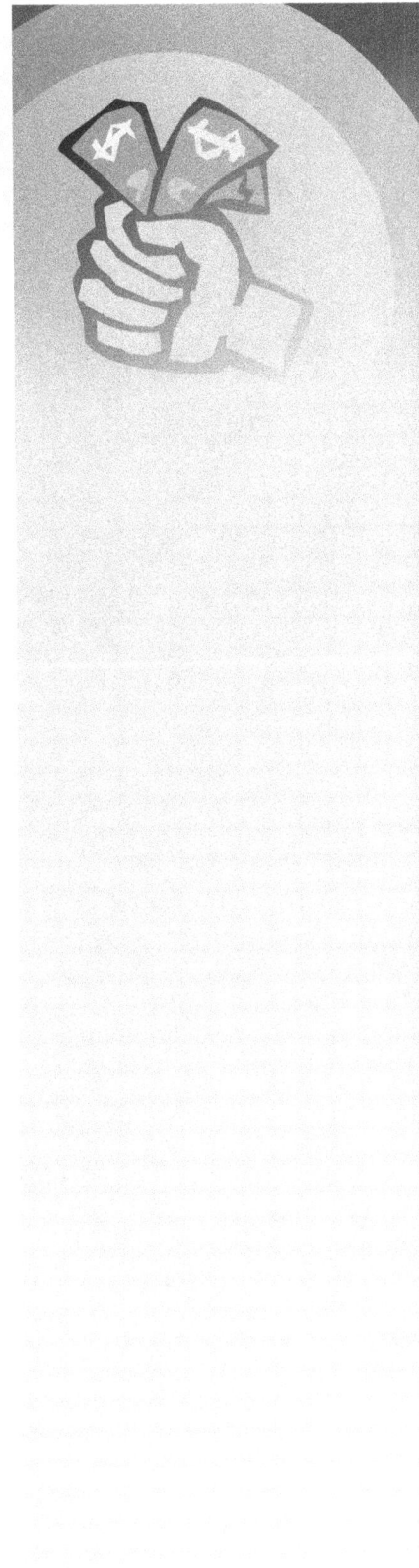

Chapter 9 Highlights

1. Adjusting one's view and approach from the seller's world to the buyer's world is the seventh Core Element of RDS.

   ### Buyer's Stages of Buying

   Evaluate Current Level of Satisfaction

   Realize a Need

   Review Options

   Sourcing Decision and Implementation

   Satisfaction After Delivery

2. Selling and servicing customers need not be a complex process, but instead a blended resource team should simply and genuinely approach everything from the Buyer's Stages of Buying.

3. RDS is trust-based. Resource teams can earn the trust of a prospect by helping them connect the dots that lead to an option, even if the option is not offered by the seller. Keeping the trust and respect should be more important than getting the sale itself. Individuals who trust and respect a resource team or team member can be valuable as ardent references in referral networking.

4. Everything in RDS is measured and guided in the buyer's world, starting and ending with the buyer's satisfaction.

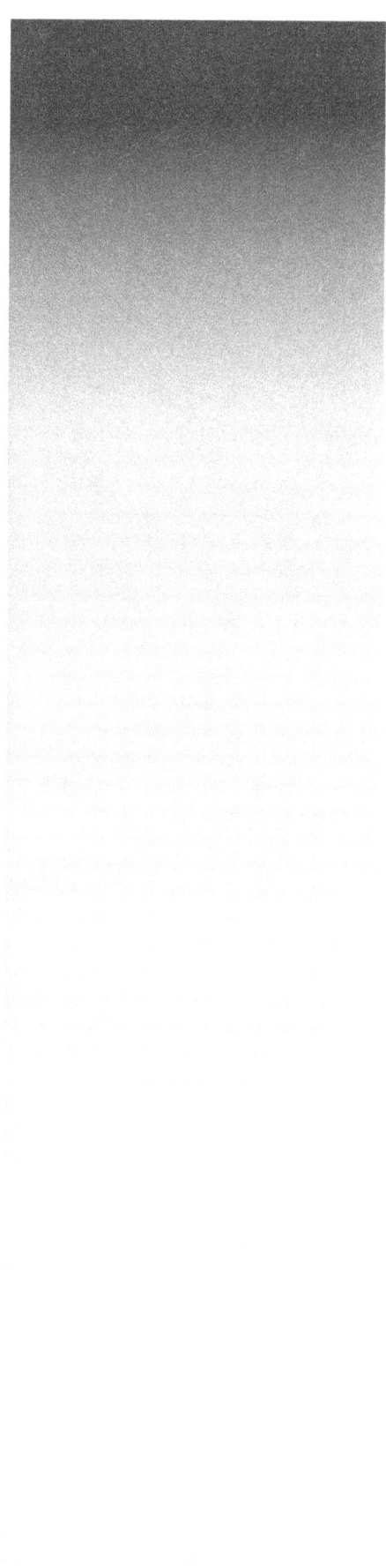

Chapter 10   Any Questions?

CHAPTER SNAPSHOT
- Asking questions can be more effective in controlling the direction of a communication
- Blending the science of asking well-planned questions with the art of adapting those questions from the customer's viewpoint

Well-Planned Questions

Because buying has replaced selling, questioning the buyer replaces telling, selling, promoting or presenting to a customer. The most essential aspect of RDS is to understand what it takes to satisfy a buyer. Developing questions, tailored to each individual buyer's behavioral style (DISC) is an art and a science each non-sales resource learns in uncovering and understanding the buyer's needs and earning their trust.

Most ineffective salespeople are known for at least one frustrating trait. Many old-style salespeople are known for being poor listeners often obsessed with their own goals and therefore, selling, telling and promoting their own viewpoint. Drilling down into these negative attributes, it appears the root of the issue is generally a lack of empathy and interest stemming from a disingenuous demeanor and constant desire to talk. Said another way, most old-style salespeople fail to ask the right questions. Some refer to this type of salesperson as a BS artist. The crux of bad selling is telling. No one likes to be told what to think or what he or she needs. When that happens, the natural instinct is usually to push back or just walk away. Planning and using questions is the most critical component of RDS and is also the eighth Core Element. Since the basic rules of selling have changed, the resulting adjustments are once again counter-intuitive and uncomfortable for most. Enter the DISC behavioral style assessment - Dominants

> *Well-planned questions can generate a genuine trust from resources who exhibit sincere empathy for the customer's situation.*

and Interactives tend to make statements or tell, while the Steadies and Compliants show more of a propensity to ask questions. The majority of salespeople we've met tend to favor the Dominant and Interactive styles and therefore, will almost always struggle with asking questions. Dominant's and Interactive's natural, fast-paced style indicates they may believe it is faster and more effective to tell people what to think than to ask them what they think. Regardless of DISC style, planning questions from the customer's point of view will almost always result in more effective communication.

What do we mean by planning questions? Planning questions for each resource to ask or preparing responses to questions the prospective customer may ask takes place during team brainstorming and call planning. Well-planned questions can generate a genuine trust from resources who exhibit sincere empathy for the customer's situation. Most people can see right through an insincere question or statement. Insincerity is generally interpreted as BS, and distrust is usually the by-product. When a prospective customer feels the resource cares more about them than closing a sale, their trust grows and natural defenses diminish. Buyer's defense occurs when the buyer forms an opinion that the seller is insincere or just out for their own benefit. That raw emotion results in the buyer either consciously or subconsciously putting up a protective barrier to keep the seller at a safe distance, preventing the

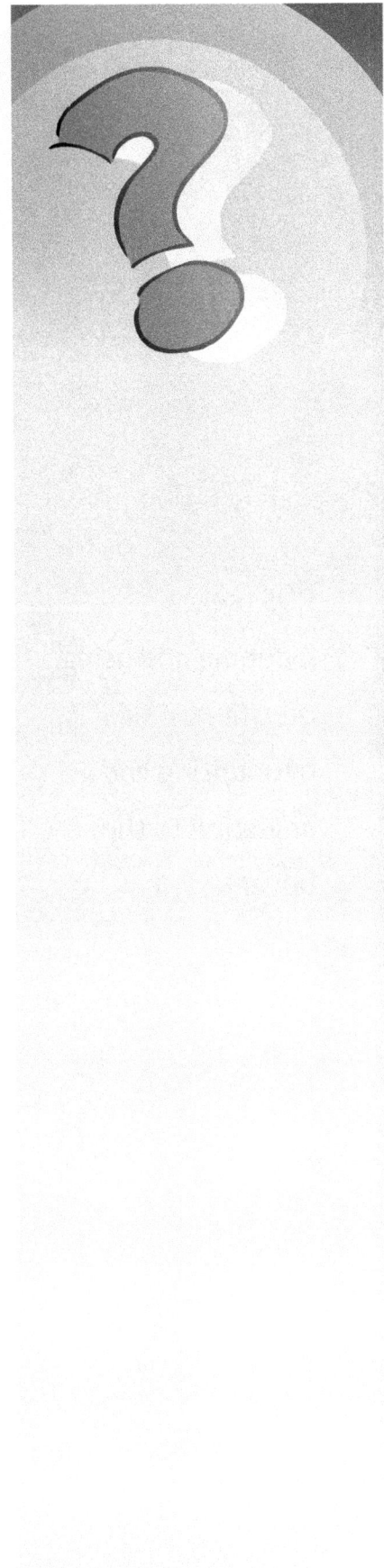

seller from actively participating in the Buyer's Stages of Buying. It is just another reason why non-sales resources can be naturally better at RDS than old-style salespeople. When paired with a potential customer by job function and DISC style, blended resource teams cannot help but be genuinely focused on learning and solving the customer's problems. Planning ensures they do not fall into the selling-and-telling mode. This increases the likelihood of a partnership because asking rehearsed questions motivates both the resource and buyer to focus on the buyer, and that behavior generates trust.

In order to help individuals who possess the natural tendency to tell, we suggest they try to listen to themselves when communicating with prospective and current customers. If your own voice is dominating the conversation, in person or on the phone, odds are you are telling, not asking questions. It may feel faster to tell, but asking questions has a much greater impact. Resources who plan and use questions can actually control the direction of the interaction without telling because they are guiding the other individual or individuals with their questions, not their pontification. The fact is, most people are poor listeners and do not hear much of what they are being told. However, most of us remember and believe more of what we hear ourselves say than what someone else tells us. It therefore can make more sense to ask questions to get the

> RDS makes planning and using questions a skill of adapting and adjusting to the buyer's style.

customer to express and remember what they talk about. If they hear themselves say, "I'd like to have a supplier that will provide more consistent delivery," won't they remember that longer than being told that better delivery is available? Also, doesn't helping the buyer verbalize their issues provide a more effective way of assisting them to connect the dots? If the buyer's answers don't generate the response the team planned for, it is possible the buyer doesn't have a need or may have a totally different need than what the team anticipated. Wouldn't you want to know that up-front before investing either party's time?

Many books have been written on how to best utilize questions, spelling out the steps or progression of questions in logical, methodical steps. The best book on utilizing both the art and science of questioning that we have read is Secrets of Question Based Selling by Thomas A. Freese because it utilizes four types of questions: diagnostic, issue, implication and solution questions.

This approach follows the natural progression of the Buyer's Stages of Buying. The level of satisfaction and need are logic-based and correspond to diagnostic and issue questions. For example, if the buyer is completely satisfied, a few diagnostic questions should quickly reveal that level of satisfaction. It can also reveal dissatisfaction as well and begin to expose the issues the buyer may be experiencing.

The buyer's evaluation of options, resolution of concerns and decision stages are more emotional than logical, and therefore align well with implication and solution questions. Question Based Selling's implication questions, or impact questions emotionally tie an impact back to each issue. These questions help the buyer connect the dots between their issues and the possible impact those issues may have on themselves and others. The emotional impact could ultimately affect the buying decision. Solution questions can tie the solution to the buyer's issues, and therefore can be more effective than telling, selling and closing. Solution statements are converted to questions designed to help the buyer filter options, address issues and arrive at an ultimate decision to buy, not to be "sold" or be "closed."

Building a relationship or revealing a need by using questions is much more than just diagnosing the issues, revealing the impact those issues have and then tying options or solutions to each issue. Using that type of logical approach is extremely helpful, but by itself, not always effective. If the science of questioning is rigidly applied without consideration of the buyer's behavioral style, the questions can actually backfire and turn a buyer off. RDS makes planning and using questions a skill of adapting and adjusting to the buyer's style. Think of it in terms of using a voltage converter for electronic devices when traveling overseas. A voltage converter adapts the energy source to

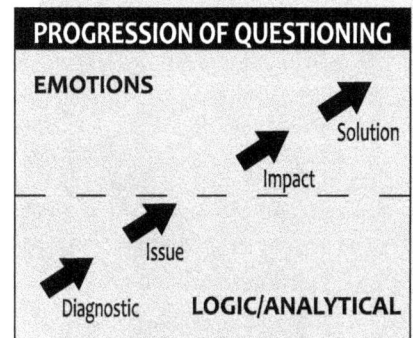

PROGRESSION OF QUESTIONING

Derived from Secrets of Question Based Selling by Thomas A. Freese – www.QBSresearch.com

fit the appliance, where the two can interrelate without causing an unexpected incident. Well planned questions can have the same affect in a communication. Questions are generated in order to convert the seller's style to the buyer's style and viewpoint, ensuring interaction without incident.

Let's look at an example of the behavioral styles impacting the logical progression of questioning. Highly Interactive DISC-style sellers can tend to create diagnostic questions from their own perspective, generally expressing how they feel, with a great deal of quick and spontaneous talking. They want to please others and be appreciated for what they do. Their questions, if asked, usually attempt to persuade others but their lack of to detail and facts in their thoughts or deeds can put them at a disadvantage. In their first interaction with a prospective buyer, they will likely jump right in and start telling the buyer about themselves, their product or service. If they formulated questions at all, those questions will be rooted in feelings and/or people. For instance, they might ask, "How do you feel about your current supplier?" or, "Are the people who work for you happy with your current supplier?" If they are lucky enough to be meeting with another Interactive style person, this approach might be an effective line of diagnostic questions that could reveal basic needs. However, if that same Interactive seller is to ask the exact same questions of a Compliant-style buyer, the result will be very different.

Compliants are very systematic individuals. Generally, they are technical individuals who focus on accuracy, will ask questions and thoroughly process data. Opinions or how others feel are not top of mind to the Compliant because they tend to use the information they have to methodically formulate a series of follow-up questions that will ultimately lead them to a precise conclusion. Compliants filter and communicate nearly the opposite way an Interactive does. Therefore, our Interactive seller will likely turn off the Compliant buyer with their questions because to the Compliant, how they feel about a supplier or whether the people who work for them are happy with a supplier has no quantifiable value in evaluating a supplier's contribution or lack thereof. Asking diagnostic questions without understanding and adapting to the buyer's DISC style may not be effective. In this example, the best way for the Interactive seller to plan for the Compliant buyer is to brainstorm with other Compliant resources on the team in order to design questions from the Compliant's viewpoint.

Blended team question planning increases the odds of successful communication with buyers simply because it is highly unlikely that all high-level decision-making buyers are fun loving, social Interactives or any single behavioral style. A quick check of the buyer's education, work experience, body language, manner of dress and office décor can give the seller, through the process of elimination, a general idea

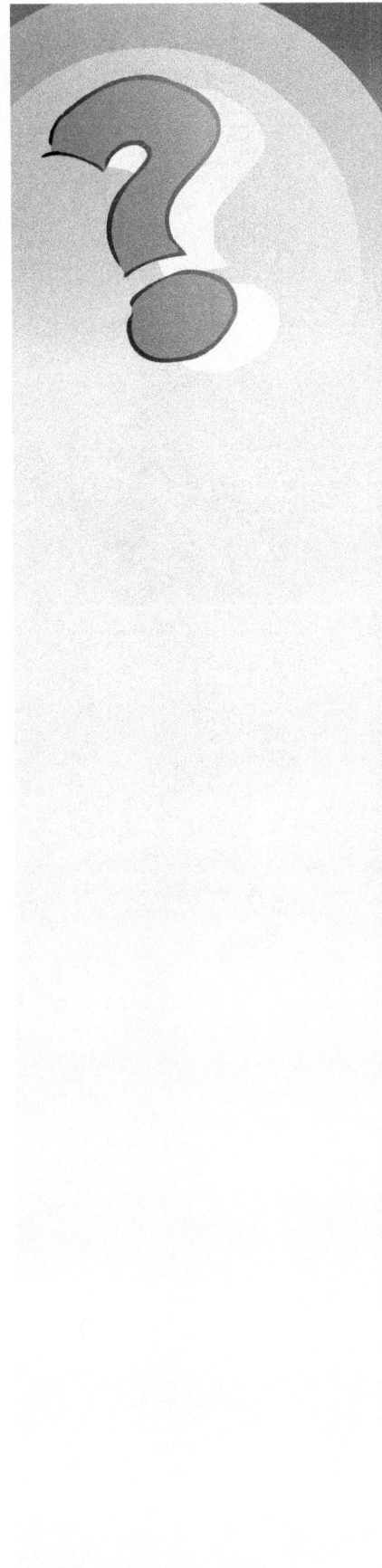

of the buyer's style. A diagnostic question such as, "Are you completely satisfied with your current supplier's product quality, delivery, service and overall value?" will play to any behavioral style. A Dominant will appreciate the directness and answer the question. An Interactive will tell you how they feel. The Steady and Compliant may ask a clarifying question or two, but eventually will be comfortable giving a logical and systematic answer. In our example, the Compliant buyer will more likely answer a well-planned diagnostic question suited to their style. It is important to note Steady and Compliant styles are typically slower to change, so a fast-paced Interactive or Dominant resource may need to employ patience when planning, asking and waiting for answers to questions.

Chapter 10 Highlights

1. The eighth Core Element, Well-Planned Questions, can build trust and therefore spark a more open relationship.

2. When communicating, if you hear your own voice more than the voices of others, odds are you are telling and not asking.

2. Consider each individual's behavioral style when developing questions .

3. Asking questions is often counter-intuitive, especially for Dominant and Interactive styles. That is why planning can minimize the natural instinct to tell and sell.

4. Telling a customer what they need or what you have does not necessarily assist the customer in connecting the dots when evaluating options. In fact, it can result in a heightened buyer's defense where they resist the seller's approach and solution, regardless of how well it fits their needs.

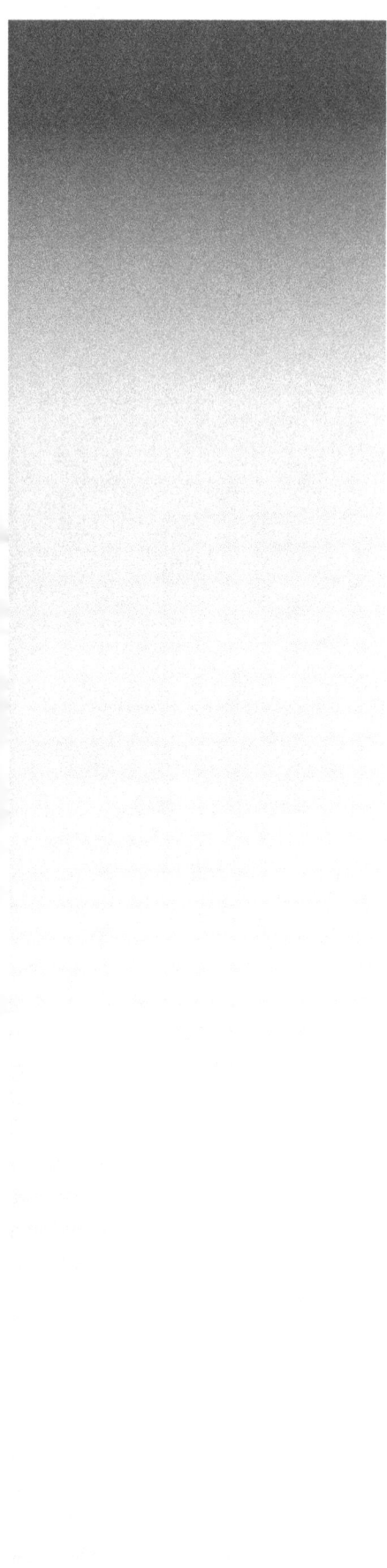

Chapter 11 Deep Dive Strategy

CHAPTER SNAPSHOT
- Researching, learning and digging deeper to plan for communication with qualified prospects
- Expanding on "known facts" uncovers and challenges the accuracy of some root strategic assumptions as the Deep Dive evolves
- Challenging each other in advance of customer communications can increase the likelihood of success

Effective RDS teams add structure to ensure effective team planning and execution. A Deep Dive is fundamental in preparing for and communicating with current and prospective customers. What is a Deep Dive? A Deep Dive is selecting a high probability prospect that has been qualified by the resource team and drilling down into what is known, assumed and not known. It is designed to prevent bad communication habits from developing and inhibiting the resource team's probability of success. Bad communication habits are generally the result of communication shortcuts. Effective communication is much like the game of golf. Most new players start with lessons, practice and the formation of good basic habits. After playing golf for a while, most stop taking lessons from a golf pro and either go out and just play or supplement their game at the driving range, potentially opening the

> *Bad communication habits are generally the result of communication shortcuts.*

CORE
ELEMENT
9

Deep Dive Strategy

A Deep Dive planning sessions utilize behavioral style assessments, business plans and pipeline trackers to create scenarios, strategies and questions based on customer styles and the Buyer's Stage of Buying. A Deep Dive serves as a guide when planning how to utilize resources in preparing, executing and following up on each and every customer communication.

door to bad habits. It wasn't until my father-in-law, a four handicap, observed the bad habits I had developed, that I was able to plot a course of correction. At first, it may be a shortcut such as rushing or muscling the golf swing a little, or adjusting the grip ever so slightly. After months of minor shortcut adjustments, a golfer can develop a well-pronounced slice that dramatically reduces his effectiveness and level of satisfaction. Generally, a few lessons with a pro can provide the much needed structure and resulting consistency for more effective and enjoyable play.

Much like the guidance provided by a golf pro, the Deep Dive relies on objective observations, critiques and suggestions of a blended resource team. The ninth Core Element of RDS is the Deep Dive Strategy, which can add structure and consistency by brainstorming and preparing for customer visits, phone calls or even chance customer meetings.

The term "Deep Dive" originated when resource teams, after identifying that a potential customer appeared to have a need, decided they needed to research, learn more or dive deeper. Thus the Deep Dive concept was initiated to guide blended and sometimes inexperienced resource teams through a better thought-out approach to planning a customer visit. It is important to note that a team Deep Dive is initiated only after a potential customer has made it through the first cut of disqualification. Customers expressing a need would qualify for a Deep Dive. Negative Planning and the resulting strategy is designed to reveal or dismiss the need altogether. The resource team dives into what is known, suspected and unknown about high probability, qualified targets that offer the greatest potential of quick close. Therefore, a Deep Dive is the resource team performing consistent in-depth analyses in order to discuss, question and plan the strategies for qualified prospects.

A Deep Dive combines facts and assumptions because in most cases only limited information is actually known for a fact. Throughout a Deep Dive, questions are asked of the prospective customer so that more and more facts are established. It is impossible to know everything a prospective or current customer needs, thinks or expects, therefore a Deep Dive encourages a resource team to logically connect known facts with educated guesses and assumptive conclusions. Refining and testing possible strategies with well planned follow up questions of each individual involved in the decision-making process helps guide the resource team in planning their next step. A call plan created by a blended resource team will generally connect the customer's needs (from the customer's viewpoint) to potential solutions much more effectively than no team plan at all.

The resource team dives into what is known, suspected and unknown about high probability, qualified targets that offer the greatest potential of a quick close.

> The Deep Dive
> approach is an
> ongoing endeavor
> where the
> brainstorming facts,
> assumptions and
> planned customer
> questioning can and
> should constantly
> change.

Elements of a Deep Dive

Brainstorming - "What We Know, What We Think We Know, What We Don't Know"

Decision and Resource Involvement Mapping - Identify all players in the customer's decision-making process and the resource team members responsible for communicating with them.

Call Planning - Strategy, Negative Planning and questioning for a customer communication based on individual behavioral styles and the Buyer's Stage of Buying.

Assess Your True Competition - Identifying the strengths and weaknesses of those the buyer considers as options.

Brainstorming

A Deep Dive cannot be accurately or fully completed in one or even two team brainstorming sessions. It usually grows in accuracy over time as the team develops, tests and refines possible scenarios, strategies and questions. The Deep Dive approach is an ongoing endeavor where the brainstorming facts, assumptions and planned customer questioning can and should constantly change. Research, questions and resource team challenges move data from what "We Don't Know" or "We Think We Know" to the ultimate goal of "We Know" for a fact. However, because

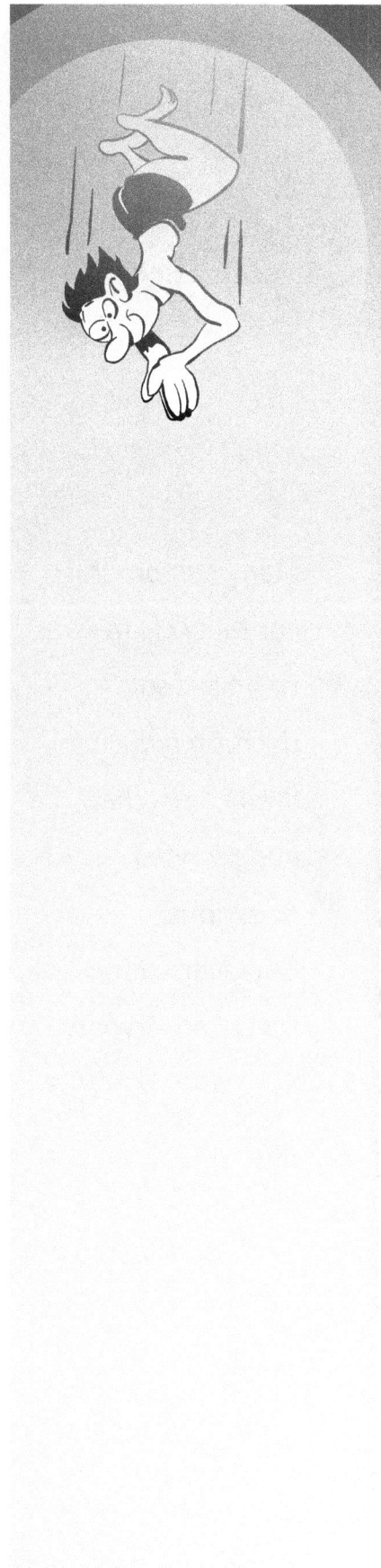

assumptions and challenges are laced throughout this approach, it is possible to go the opposite way as well. For instance, early in the discovery process, data, which the team thought to be factual, can become uncertain, as additional data is considered, debated and challenged.

I remember a client who swore that he was dealing with the ultimate decision maker of a privately held prospective customer. Based on our client's insistence that his contact was indeed the sole decision maker and approver, we built a month long series of strategic Deep Dive customer visit call plans, phone calls and follow up questions on what we believed to be a fact. However, in order to continuously challenge our assumption that we were dealing with the ultimate decision maker and approver, we asked the prospect a series of questions over time. The first question was "If you were to decide to do business with us, would you actually be the one signing the contract?" When he replied "Yes," we continued our planning with him as the primary target however, after a team review of the "facts," several resources began to cast doubt and criticism on the team's first question. The team decided a second, more refined question should be asked since it was doubtful this prospective $200 million customer left the approval and vendor decision to just one individual. Our second question was, "What is your decision-making process and is there any affiliation with the chain of private hospitals

> *Many customer contacts claim to be the sole decision maker. Well-researched and planned questions, however, can reveal otherwise.*

listed on your website?" We had finally asked the question that would help us accurately connect the facts and remove the erroneous assumptions we had made. It was a fact that this approver and decision maker signed the contracts however, the hospital's board of directors controlled 60% of the company. Therefore, this gentleman was actually an influencer and a recommender as well as a decision maker and approver because we discovered he could not sign a contract unless the board of a separate, outside organization granted him the authority to do so. That new fact changed the direction of the planning process.

Many customer contacts claim to be the sole decision maker. Well-researched and planned questions, however, can reveal otherwise. The players involved in a decision-making process can change, causing known "facts" to get re-categorized to "We Think We Know" or "We Don't Know" for sure anymore. This entire method may sound time consuming or even maddening, but it has just the opposite effect when learning customer needs and differentiating a team from the competition. Challenging one another prior to a customer visit actually makes the team better informed and prepared for that customer interaction. Information is power, but in this case, the power comes from knowing more than is assumed. Resource teams communicate more confidently when they do so from the customer's viewpoint and with facts logically connected to informed assumptions. The team's brainstorming inspires resource team confidence because it removes most of the erroneous and unknown data before meeting with a prospective customer, not in front of the customer. It also provides a degree of credibility, as the customer discovers something different about this team – perhaps they listened and did their homework!

Doing what is easy, taking shortcuts and/or following what most others do isn't always the best thing to do. In fact, most of the inventions and discoveries that improve how things are done have occurred because they were different, difficult and counter to what the majority believed. Sometimes the awkward or difficult things people avoid in life are the very things they need to consider. For me, one of those things is healthier high fiber food such as black beans, lentils and oatmeal. I'm told, at my age that I must consider eating more high fiber foods because they are good for me, but I don't because they usually provide me with embarrassing and often uncontrollable moments in public. Perhaps a more suitable example of beneficial, but awkward things comes from something I recently heard my pastor say. He said that his faith grew more when he forced himself to seek teachings and opinions that were diametrically opposed to those he held. He went on to say that challenging the very beliefs that he holds dear actually opened his eyes to discussing and considering things he

> *It also provides a degree of credibility, as the customer discovers something different about this team-- perhaps they listened and did their homework!*

would not have in the past. He explained that this approach does not weaken or threaten his knowledge, but actually strengthens it, because it forces him to openly consider other points of view that he would not otherwise have even thought of. Additionally, he said that challenging and questioning beliefs are healthy, even necessary, in expanding knowledge. It made sense to me that when an individual locks in on what they believe, they remove all doubt from their mind. However, removing doubt does not necessarily eliminate the chances of being misinformed or being wrong. My pastor simply invites both shared and differing viewpoints in order to come closer to discovering the truth.

I remember thinking how different my pastor's approach was to those of other priests, pastors and spiritual leaders. I assumed that most religious leaders studied, practiced and discussed their specific doctrine primarily with those who shared their same point of view. I thought that perhaps they kept a watchful eye on those who disagreed or believed in something different, but for the most part, they surrounded themselves with those who agreed with them. However, after challenging my viewpoint and reflecting on the counter-intuitive mindset my pastor spoke of, I realized that the truth is especially difficult to find until you allow and encourage others to challenge you.

When I was sitting in the service that Sunday, it hit me

like a ton of bricks that my mind was wandering again and that I was thinking about this book. What I realized was that the RDS facts, or the "What We Know" data, are similar to the truth my pastor was looking for. True facts can be hidden beneath confusing and conflicting details, opinions and misinformation, and then that data can be filtered even further in order to force it to fit into a comfortable package we can believe in. Brainstorming, questioning, Negative Planning and challenging the data brings us closer to realizing the facts, and therefore establishing a trust-based relationship with a customer. I then had two revelations right there in church. The first was that I'd better pay attention to the pastor and stop daydreaming about this book, and the second was that it may seem frustrating and counterproductive to invite opposing viewpoints, but if we don't, we may never successfully understand, plan and approach things from the buyer's viewpoint. So, the Deep Dive method of challenging may be maddening and counter-intuitive, but it is not unproductive. When properly executed, a Deep Dive brainstorming approach positions a blended resource team to take the next step of planning the customer communication.

We've already examined the concept of Negative Planning. Challenging what is known, assumed, and not known through Negative Planning is the foundation for the Deep Dive planning approach. Let's look at what Deep

> *Brainstorming, questioning, Negative Planning and challenging the data brings us closer to the facts.*

Dive Decision Mapping and Call Planning can provide for the team.

Decision and Resource Involvement Mapping

A Decision Map provides the basis for what we need to know before developing a strategy or customer visit plan. We strongly advise not to take shortcuts on this aspect of the Deep Dive. Questions and strategies are developed, altered and adjusted around the individuals involved in the decision-making process (described in Chapter 5).

Building a Decision Map

Strive to get factual answers to these questions:

-What is the decision-making process and timeline?
-Who are the approvers and decision makers?
-Who are the users, influencers and recommenders?
-Who are the potential blockers we may encounter?
-What are the DISC behavioral styles of everyone identified?
-What is driving their behaviors and what are their needs, issues and concerns?
-What role will they play in the overall decision?
-Where are they in the Buyer's Stage of Buying?
-What does the resource team need to do to successfully address the needs, issues and concerns for each individual?

Keep in mind the answers to these questions will result not only from specific questions asked of all those involved in the decision process, but also verbal and non-verbal observations made by the resources during their interactions with these individuals.

The answers will likely be inconsistent and incomplete, but the blended resource team's task is to logically piece together the people, facts and assumptions into a Decision Map. Once the pieces are in place, the team compares, contrasts and challenges the data collected at all levels, ensuring the most accurate assessment of the customer's decision-making process. The resource team must diligently challenge themselves to uncover every possible player (page 96). Keep in mind that players can be visible or unseen and often come from within or even outside of the customer's organization. Blockers, such as "silent partners" or former associates, may have opinions that can derail your team's efforts. Direct and often difficult questions must be developed to ensure that these potentially devastating players are revealed and their issues addressed. Even if the resource team remotely suspects the slightest potential issue, prepare a few questions to intentionally force the issue to the surface. Not doing so could submarine the team later down the road, wasting months of effort in the pursuit of the customer.

> *The resource team must diligently challenge themselves to uncover every possible player.*

> *Understanding the resources' significant strengths and potential weaknesses sets the team up for the most appropriate interactions with the potential customer.*

Once the buyer's Decision Map is created, the resource team needs to build their own Resource Involvement Map to balance the resource team.

Creating a Resource Involvement Map

For each resource:
- List their title and role in your organization
- Determine their DISC behavioral style
- Understand their strengths, value and role in the strategy

Understanding the resources' significant strengths and potential weaknesses sets the team up for the most appropriate interactions with the potential customer.

In the game of football, the strategy is to have a team balanced in speed, strength and agility to diffuse the strengths and exploit the weaknesses of the other team. For instance, you would more likely place your fastest defensive player opposite the other's team's fastest wide receiver. Likewise, you'll probably want to put your biggest, agile lineman up against their strongest defensive lineman. Additionally, making substitutions to counter unexpected changes should be part of the strategy. The Resource Involvement Map, when compared to the customer's Decision Map, will help placement of resources. Deploying a highly accurate and detailed billing coordinator with a demanding CFO who requires specific evidence and guarantees is arguably a better strategy than taking a personable, empathetic customer service individual and expecting them to provide the CFO with the detail and in-depth examples he or she requires. Improper resource-customer alignment can result in failure for both parties, unless the assigned resource is thoroughly prepared with a detailed call plan that includes objectives, questions and strategies that adequately address the behavioral style and point of view of the customer.

Call Planning

Once the Decision and Resource Involvement Maps are established, the team can best develop an effective call plan. A call plan will dictate the strategy and tactics to achieve the strategy. Every phone call, face-to-face or chance meeting should have a pre-determined purpose and expected meeting length. Chance meetings can and should be planned in case they occur. One of the most embarrassing experiences in my professional career was when I forgot a CFO's name during a change encounter on my way to a meeting with someone else in his building! Thinking lightening couldn't strike twice, I was again graced with his presence on my next visit and again, I drew a blank on his name. Call it memory lapse or lack of attention to detail, but in the end, I had not planned on the interaction,

> *Every phone call, face-to-face or chance meeting should have a pre-determined purpose and expected meeting length.*

> *Many teams prepare the plan to accommodate for last-minute changes at the hands of the prospective customer.*

and therefore I filled my mind with other thoughts and concerns and was caught off guard. After that second chance meeting, it was easy to surmise the CFO was not one of my fans. From that point on I learned to make a point of reviewing the list of the names of anyone I might run into and plan a brief comment just in case I do run into one of them.

Elements of a Call Plan

- Meeting Length
- Purpose
- Objectives
- Questions

Meeting Length: Does the time allocated for the meeting provide ample time to cover the team priorities set forth? How much time is available for the resource team? What can be accomplished in 15 minutes vs. two hours can alter the call plan priorities or even uncover that the team will need to request additional time to accomplish the tasks at hand. Many teams prepare the plan to accommodate for last-minute changes at the hands of the prospective customer. Should the meeting length change at the last minute, the call plan can be adjusted on the fly by prioritizing the objectives and questions, providing flexibility to skip less important content in favor of accomplishing the overall objective.

Purpose: Always have a clear purpose for any phone call or visit to a customer or prospective customer, thus providing them some kind of value, or at least approaching the conversation from their perspective. Nothing can upset busy buyers more than vendors who provide a vague response to the question "What is the purpose of your visit?" Answers such as "I was in the area" could get the buyer wondering if you stopped by to use the bathroom, and since you had to pass by his office, thought you'd stop and say hello to him. The purpose must be precise and measurable in terms of what is to be accomplished, but above all else, it must present a value for the customer. Plan the purpose of your call ahead of time: "I'd like to spend our time today to clarify your time line and decision-making process for the ABC project. As soon as I clearly understand your needs and expectations, I can provide you with the delivery details and pricing that you need. Is there anything else you'd like to cover today?" If the joint expectations are in sync, take the opportunity to reconfirm the meeting length by asking "We have 60 minutes set aside for today's discussion, does that still fit with your schedule?" If the meeting is shortened, adjust the call plan asking only the highest priority questions (prepared ahead of time). Be diligent adhering to the time allotted, and prepare to stop when the customer's time is exhausted. It is better to end the visit on time than to attempt to get answers to all of your planned questions. In many cases, the buyer will have

> *The purpose must be precise and measurable in terms of what is to be accomplished, but above all else, it must present a value for the customer.*

> *The heart and soul of the call plan lies in the questioning segment.*

mentally moved on to his or her next scheduled item, so don't assume continuing is beneficial unless the buyer says so.

Objectives: Next in the Call Plan is to create call objectives specifically for the resource team, not for the customer. The customer should already understand the meeting's purpose if you properly established that when setting the meeting up. Objectives should be specific and measurable by the resource team and should be designed to qualify or disqualify a prospect. Avoid soft, subjective, vague or difficult to measure objectives, such as "build a relationship." Focus on more direct objectives, such as, "identify the decision-making process to include all board level approvers and executive level decision makers." For instance, if the objective is to identify the decision-making process, the outcome of the meeting will have produced a clear and measureable understanding of the decision-making process. At the very least, the team will have a better understanding of the facts, placing a focus on subsequent objectives to be achieved.

Questions: The heart and soul of the call plan lies in the questioning segment. Questioning is both an art and a science and goes beyond information gathering by controlling the direction of a discussion and encouraging the buyer to see your point of view as you guide them to verbalize answers to your questions.

The Art and Science of Questioning

Applying the correct type of question:
- Diagnostic
- Issue
- Impact
- Solution

At the right time in the Buyer's Stage of Buying:
- Evaluate Current Level of Satisfaction
- Realize a Need
- Review Options
- Sourcing Decision and Implementation
- Satisfaction After Delivery

While adapting to the individual's DISC style:
- Dominant
- Interactive
- Steady
- Compliant

When it comes to following a RDS Deep Dive call plan methodology, combining both art and science take practice and discipline. It will not happen over night or without effort to change old communication habits. That is why RDS is a team effort where individuals challenge other team members to learn and then follow the team's

> *Short cuts and 'winging it' will seldom be as effective as well-planned questions.*

plan. Questions that effectively hit the desired mark take time to develop. Short cuts and "winging it" will seldom be as effective as well-planned questions. Stay away from generic questions, and opt for specific questions tailored to each individual. You can and should triangulate - ask the same question of two or three people to verify or clarify a reply - but don't ask two or more people the same list of questions, simply because each individual you talk to has a unique DISC behavioral style, job responsibility, concerns and expectations. No single list of questions can draw out every possible combination of style, responsibility and personal expectation, so attempting to do so with a rigid list of standard questions will appear contrived.

Reviewing the "We Know," "We Think We Know" and "We Don't Know" brainstorming data with pipeline comments will reveal an outline of a rough plan and likely scenario, or at the very least the missing pieces to the plan. The missing pieces dictate the very questions that need to be asked. Call plan objectives and missing data become the road map for a phone call or customer meeting. That data is the basis for creating initial questions, designed to uncover or confirm. Once asked, the information received feeds the facts and educated guesses already established, only now you can logically connect the dots with fewer presumptions and unknowns. In other words, the answers will begin to guide your team in knowing if you can really satisfy the customer.

Questions should be tailored to each individual customer's DISC style because in the words of Henry Ford, "If there is any one secret of success, it lies in the ability to get the other person's point of view and see things from that person's angle as well as from your own." Therefore, constant referral to the Decision Map is necessary. For instance, questions asked of Dominant style customers are best if they are direct and focus on results. Dominants want to get to the point and skip the small talk, which is quickly dismissed as unnecessary. In fact, consider starting at the end with a question such as, "Bottom line, what is it you want to walk away with today?" That approach would likely be less effective for the other styles. Interactive style people thrive on the happy, personal small talk. Many can fill up an entire meeting with small talk and never accomplish anything quantifiable; they just "feel" as if the meeting went well. They like to be asked about their feelings and opinions and who they think needs to be involved in future discussions. Interactives would respond well to "Tell me how you feel this issue is impacting the people in your department?" If dealing with a Steady, focus on questions that seek to address the logical step-by-step, check-the-box tasks that must be done. They do not appreciate a direct style question or a question that pressures them to make a decision without taking time to review the options. Compliant style people are more task-oriented, and because they want to take their time to consider the detail available,

Many can fill up an entire meeting with small talk and never accomplish anything quantifiable; they just "feel" as if the meeting went well.

> *If you don't have time to do it right the first time, what makes you think you'll have time to do it again?*

they are not very receptive to direct questions either. This behavioral approach to developing questions may seem intimidating at first, but we have found that most resources engage quickly once they understand the basic DISC behavioral style patterns. The art and science of developing questions from the individual customer's DISC style takes time, however, the more questions are planned and tested the more proficient one becomes. I once heard someone ask, "If you don't have time to do it right the first time, what makes you think you'll have the time to do it again?" Investing the time and planning the right questions can actually save time. Not only can it reduce the number of questions that need to be asked, it also can help avoid wasting time asking insignificant questions that are often the result of winging it. RDS may take an investment in team planning upfront but it generally results in fewer, more productive and successful customer interactions.

A team review of the call plan objectives and the brainstorming data is an ideal place to begin question formulation. Create, categorize and prioritize a list of topics to serve as the basis for the questions, from what the team doesn't know and thinks they know to filling in missing or unstable data in order to achieve the team's call objectives. In all cases, identify and continually qualify the players in the decision-making process who can provide accurate answers. Keep in mind, the questions are customized to confirm or dispel said "facts" as well as provide answers to what is not known. Again, this is accomplished from the customer's DISC style point of view, so before actually designing questions, the resources asking the questions should be matched up with participants in the decision-making process with similar DISC styles. A quick comparison of the buyer's Decision Map with the Resource Involvement Map can help determine the right resource match. Those best suited to deliver the team-generated questions and strategies are also determined according to their DISC styles and job responsibilities. Both buyer and seller are analyzed to determine which resources best compliment and balance the target buyer's styles, issues, needs, job responsibilities and the customer's readiness to share their needs and concerns. To determine the most appropriate questions to ask, refer to the four types of questions.

Once the questions to be asked are created by the team, the focus switches to preparation of questions the prospective customer may ask of the team. The quickest way to accurately accomplish this is to think of all the features and benefits of your company's product or service and prepare questions that you have been asked by others in the past as well as logical questions you would ask if you were a prospective customer. With proper team planning, one can highlight the advantages of either perceived positives or perceived negatives. For example, if

> *Those best suited to deliver the team-generated questions and strategies are also determined according to their DISC styles and job responsibilities.*

> *Brainstorm the worst-case scenario; the questions that could be asked, but you pray will never come up.*

one knows from experience that being the largest publicly owned company in the industry is viewed as both a plus and an obstacle, prepare an answer either way. The resource team member being asked the question might say, "Being the largest in the industry provides us with economies of scale in buying and securing services such as low cost transportation based on volume contracts. To what extent is it important to you to do business with the lowest cost provider who is able to pass savings on to you?" Said another way, "You've met our local team, do you feel more secure dealing with a small team of locally involved people with the backing of a large, growing corporation solidly behind them, or a regional group that might be limited by access to resources and capital?"

Brainstorm the worst-case scenario; the questions that could be asked, but you pray will never come up. As a team, simply list of all the negatives that competitors, former employees and angry customers think or say about the company, products and services. Next, consider other issues that have been or should be swept under the carpet. If there has been a well-publicized product recall or lawsuit don't hide from it. Plan on any of those thoughts becoming a possible question that may be asked. To prevent a "deer in the headlights" reaction, preplan logical, non-emotional responses to keep in control of the communication.

It was obvious that our client's entire customer facing team was paralyzed with fear.

Perhaps the best way to illustrate this is by sharing a true experience. Several years ago, we were targeting distressed clients who needed help, so we signed a client who had filed for Chapter 11 bankruptcy protection two weeks prior to our first facilitated training session for their sales and technical teams. Everything was going just fine until one of the salespeople asked, "What should we do when customers talk about our Chapter 11?" He went on to tell us that the competition was having a field day suggesting liquidation or worse and as a result the salesman had not made a sales call in two weeks because he didn't know what to say. Nearly everyone in the room echoed the sentiment. It was obvious that our client's entire customer facing team was paralyzed with fear. This was a perfect time to not only discuss when to negative plan for questions that will be asked, but also how to put a happy face on a pile of manure. We told them if they were asked that type of question, the worst thing they could do was to go turtle and pull their head into their shell. That is exactly what the competition and some sadistic customers want to accomplish. We told the room full of paralyzed customer-facing professionals to plan not only to show that they have no fear at all, but also to look as though the question just made their day. We advised them to take advantage of body language, leaning forward in the chair and with a big smile saying "I am so glad you brought that up! Chapter 11 is quite possibly the best thing that could have happened to our company. Did you know that it will

> *Throughout this evolution, the seller's "Lead Dog" resource can and should change often.*

allow us to become a stronger and better supplier since it will enable us to renegotiate our leases, our labor contracts and work with our lenders and creditors to reduce our costs? It is helping us to shed ancillary businesses so we can concentrate on improving the productivity, quality, service and overall value of our core competencies, something I am very excited about for our company's future. Like I said, I'm glad you asked, because this Chapter 11 will benefit both of us!" The sales and technical team could not wait to get back out in front of their customers because they felt prepared for even the nastiest of questions.

As stated earlier, a call plan is not a single point of customer contact. Over time, after numerous phone calls and meetings, a relationship will evolve and deepen toward resolving the prospective customer's issues. Throughout this evolution, the seller's "Lead Dog" resource can and should change often. In other words, the traditional method of deploying a single sales rep to make all customer contacts is keeping the lead dog stagnant. In order to best compliment the various players in the decision-making process, it is foolish to believe that any single individual can successfully communicate with everyone. As illustrated earlier in our example, old-style salespeople often refuse to relinquish their position as the lead dog, because doing so means they would give up control. RDS encourages individual resources to impact only the components for which they are best qualified and step aside when a different pairing has a higher likelihood of success for a particular task or objective. In fact, no single resource is capable of consistently interacting and negotiating with every type of buyer, especially when one considers the emotionally energized situations they could find themselves in. The term "personality conflict" refers to the fact that people do not always successfully communicate with or get along with everyone. In reality, personality conflicts are more common than not, because people naturally tend to communicate with others from their own perspective, not the other person's perspective. Some people are more effective at communicating than others, which is why the RDS lead dog changes as necessary to provide the best possible conditions to communicate and build trust.

After the Decision and Resource Involvement Maps have been analyzed, the resources properly aligned and those executing the plan have been challenged to ensure that the right team has been selected, the call plan is ready to be executed. As stated earlier, the call plan starts by designating when the meeting, call or dialogue will take place, how long the session is scheduled to last and who on both sides may be involved. The Decision Map will have already provided guidance in detailing the styles, needs and strategies for each individual along with the resource best suited to handle a particular individual involved in the decision-making

> *In reality, personality conflicts are more common than not, because people naturally tend to communicate with others from their own perspective.*

> *Everything about RDS minimizes the possibility of failing.*

process. The expected duration of the interaction must be taken into consideration when listing the call objectives and the questions to ask as well as questions that may be asked of the team, prioritizing from most to least important. In the true style of Negative Planning, preparing the resource team to prioritize the most important questions will provide a safety net for any unexpected change of plans, especially if the meeting time suddenly changes from 1-hour to 15 minutes.

Everything about RDS minimizes the possibility of failing. The call plan is no exception because it focuses on unpleasant and uncomfortable issues that old school salespeople instinctively ignore. However, these issues, if ignored can be catastrophic. RDS resources should respectfully challenge each other during brainstorming to gain consensus on how to encourage the buyer to introduce all obstacles. Doing so early on lessens the possibility of jeopardizing mutual trust at any point in the relationship. We have found that the majority of failed pursuits occurred at the hands of someone who elected to hide or ignore someone or something that should have been properly addressed.

For example, one of our early clients asked us to help their sales and service team to secure a new customer. The salesperson heading the effort claimed to have everything

"under control" because he had good relationship with the Purchasing Agent (PA) who, according to him was the only important point of contact. Identifying a classic red flag in RDS, we knew that more than just the salesperson needed to be involved. The newly assembled resource team consisted of a timid bunch of customer service people and therefore lacked true cross-functionality. After some fundamental brainstorming challenges from us, it became obvious that the salesman didn't know the PA's supervisor or any of the senior level decision makers. When pushed, he reverted to his handy excuse that the executives were "silent partners," and they refused to grant salespeople access. At our prodding, the resource team suggested one of the company's executives reach out to a silent partner or two with a phone call. The salesman dismissed that idea and every other idea as a waste of time. He decided to ignore the fact that he did not know the ultimate decision makers and approvers because he was comfortable with his sole contact, the PA. We were unsuccessful in convincing the salesman to invite other resources in and allow RDS to work. He ultimately lost that opportunity. Several months later he lost his job. The open nature of RDS encourages resources to challenge each other in an effort to reveal as many facts and missing pieces as possible. If properly implemented, RDS would have removed that salesman as the lead dog and at the very least would have categorized the seller's lack of relationship with the buyer's decision

> *The open nature of RDS encourages resources to challenge each other in an effort to reveal as many facts and missing pieces as possible.*

makers and approvers as a red flag or a low likelihood. Low likelihood prospects are not pursued until relationships are established at all levels of the customer's organization.

Assess Your True Competition

> *Current and prospective customers choose other vendors because they feel that another option presents a better value.*

Current and prospective customers choose other vendors because they feel that another option presents a better value. In other words, sellers often lose because another "option" eliminates them. Consider conducting a Competitive Analysis, a summary of the strengths and weakness of competitors. It is really nothing more than an objective way for a seller to know other options available to the buyer. Remember knowledge is power. Most times securing the knowledge that a competitor is a better fit for a prospective customer is one of those uncomfortable facts that a seller sweeps under the rug with his happy ears. Many old-style salespeople abuse, hide from or filter this harsh reality because they do not want to admit that some competitors offer customers a better value than they do. When a salesperson asks, "who else is bidding this project" and the buyer replies "XYZ and LMN" an old-style salesperson tends to bad mouth XYZ and LMN. This cannot only have a negative impact on the customer's trust, it can also result in making an entire seller's organization appear classless. The old adage of "what you don't know, can't hurt you" is far from true in the buyer/seller relationship. All the good, bad and ugly facts about your competitors need to be objectively known in order to truly understand the customer's options and your true strengths and weaknesses.

Knowing the competition and therefore approaching the customer's options from the customer's viewpoint needs to be taken into account when developing call plan objectives and questions. If a competitor offers significantly better pricing, but their quality, service and delivery are not as good as yours, does that knowledge change the line of questioning? It should! Questions that help quantify the cost and impact of poor service, poor quality and late deliveries on overall price (especially when directed at those responsible for operations and finance), may actually negate the competitor's price advantage without ever bad mouthing them. When sellers badmouth a competitor, they run the risk of eroding their credibility. Well-planned questions can lead a buyer to a quantifiable conclusion that one seller's option provides more value than the competition.

> "All the good, bad and ugly facts about your competitors need to be known in order to truly understand the customers' options."

Chapter 11 Highlights

1. The ninth Core Element, the *Deep Dive Strategy*, consists of Brainstorming, Decision and Resource Involvement Mapping, Call Planning and Competitive Analysis, and is directly linked to planning, Negative Planning and questioning based on Buyer's Stage of Buying and behavioral styles.

2. Brainstorm and plan for a customer interaction from meeting length to the actual questions to ask.

3. A Decision Map can provide a resource team with the foundation to develop a strategy and highlights the behavioral styles and perceived issues of the players in the decicion-making process.

4. The Deep Dive guides the resource team in all aspects of planning, including who to involve and how to involve them as well as the plan, execution and follow up for each customer communication. It is the road map to ensure everything begins and ends from the buyer's point of view.

5. The content of the Deep Dive grows and increases in value over time. It is not a one-time planning session.

6. It is more important to prove your own assumptions wrong early on than to be surprised months into a pursuit. It may not be what you want to hear, but it is the best for all involved.

7. Truths and facts are difficult to uncover unless challenged by others to question what one knows, thinks or assumes.

8. An objective Competitive Assessments can help the team capitalize on your company's strengths and minimize your weaknesses OR capitalize on your competitor's weaknesses and minimize their strengths.

The Execution of RDS

Chapter 12   Retention Feeds Growth

CHAPTER SNAPSHOT
• Realizing that by design, RDS begins with growth pursuits to encourage a blended resource team to adopt good planning and communication habits that ultimately lead to a continuous cycle of retention that feeds growth.

So far, our primary focus has been on new customer growth. That's because most non-sales resources are relatively secure in the knowledge that properly performing their daily tasks contributes directly or indirectly to servicing current customers. In other words, they are already fairly comfortable performing the daily tasks that ultimately contribute to creating and delivering products and services that retain customers, even if they seldom, if ever, actually interact directly with a customer. If non-sales resources were asked to embrace a new, counter-intuitive service, manufacturing or quality approach, they may resist much like some old-style salespeople resist RDS. However, RDS doesn't challenge non-sales resources to stop what they do; it encourages them to do their daily job with an emphasis on expanding their responsibilities by also communicating directly with the customer.

Almost any resource experienced in following a long-standing approach will tend to have difficulty accepting change, especially significant change. Many old-style

> *Almost any resource experienced in following a long-standing approach will tend to have difficulty accepting change, especially significant change.*

> *Prospective customers want to know how current customers are treated.*

salespeople view RDS as significant change because it challenges nearly everything they know. This book wasn't meant to exclude salespeople; however, most old-style salespeople will resist the sweeping change required to successfully approach selling 100% from the buyer's perspective, utilizing a blended resource group. Non-sales resources are more receptive to RDS and open to learning how to build and maintain consistent customer relationships from the customer's viewpoint and based on trust, not on cheesy sales gimmicks.

Introducing the non-sales resources first to RDS new customer development and later transitioning to RDS retention is intentional. When non-sales resources are initially involved in RDS customer growth, and experience modest success and the resulting confidence, they tend to quickly parallel RDS growth with RDS customer retention as new habits and skill sets are being developed. New communication skills learned in prospecting, no matter how small, boost confidence when applied to the more familiar current customer retention activities already ingrained in non-sales resources. Happy current customers not only make excellent references, but the improved customer trust and satisfaction can become a marketing tool to genuinely illustrate how the resource team consistently services their satisfied customers. Prospective customers want to know how current customers are treated. A satisfied customer

base is a credible source of new customer confidence because actual examples of how a seller's product or service performs is much more important than being told by the seller how they feel they perform. As consumers, we not only research a product or service before we buy it, but we also actively look for consumer reviews. Many consumers actually look at the negative comments first, wondering, "What's the worst it could be?" As options are disqualified, the buyer moves on to a more intense review of the qualified options.

Retention, or customer loyalty needs to be viewed internally as the standard both current and prospective customers will use as a qualifier/disqualifier because buying has very little to do with what the seller says, but has everything to do with what customers say the seller does. If the perception of the seller is consistently positive, buyers will be more likely to consider the seller as an option. When the seller's resource team understands that it is the buyer buying, not the seller selling, the sales pressure is eliminated. This philosophy also acts as a differentiator, as many salespeople still view their job as selling, not just helping the buyer buy. As the old school sellers fail to secure new business, they scratch their heads, not fully understanding that continuing to sell in a buyer's world can set them and their company up for failure! The best plan for new customer growth is retention fed growth because it

As options are disqualified, the buyer moves on to a more intense review of the qualified options.

encourages the buyer to buy and the seller's resource team to service and provide solutions.

Chapter 12 Highlights

1. Although the primary focus of this book has been new customer growth, the planning, questioning and communication elements that feed growth are the very same that enhance retention.
2. Testimony from current customers can be more impactful than a seller's actions.
3. Buyers buy, sellers shouldn't sell. Assist the buyer with buying.
4. Customer retention is the main component in successful new customer growth.

CHAPTER SNAPSHOT
• Reflecting back on what didn't work, when and why prepares the team for future sucess.

Remove the Possibility of Failure, Even When RDS Itself Fails

Conducting a Postmortem after a failed pursuit reinforces the resource team's confidence that they can prevail in the future by reviewing and pinpointing the actions that were either improperly executed or ignored altogether.

As Chris and I fine-tuned and improved the first RDS methodology, we began to see a pattern that because not every new customer pursuit or current customer retention attempt ended triumphantly, many of the resources felt they had contributed to the failure. This was the basis of our third Epiphany, if the risk of failure is removed from RDS, the risk of failure for each individual also has to be removed, not just concealed or swept under the rug. This is not as difficult as it sounds.

Because RDS is a resource team approach that utilizes individual strengths, the resource team is blended and aligned according to their DISC behavioral style and work responsibility with the players in the decision-making process. Additionally, RDS requires that resources be switched in or out of the stream of communication with the customer depending on the situation. RDS requires that the entire resource team brainstorm and plan their actions and reactions based on a very logical customer-

CORE ELEMENT 10

The Postmortem

A Postmortem is a resource team's critique of what went wrong when attempting to secure or maintain a customer. A Postmortem is not a management critique or a review of any of the individual people involved. Errors in accurately collecting, categorizing and interpreting facts from the customer's viewpoint are identified and assessed in a Postmortem. This approach removes the last possible chance that a non-sales resource can fail when participating in a resource-driven approach.

centric focus. Therefore, when RDS fails to net the desired outcome, the team needs to understand why.

Scrutiny of what goes wrong in RDS is referred to as a Postmortem, our 10th and final Core Element. The best way to illustrate what a RDS Postmortem does is to ask oneself a few questions.

• Have I ever been surprised when a potential customer chooses a different option than mine?

• Why is it that immediately after learning that an opportunity is lost that the light bulb goes on and you are keenly aware of the obvious signals that foretold of the outcome?

Take the RDS methodology one step further by applying the principles of the Postmortem during a pursuit to help a team clearly and objectively Negative Plan and avoid a potential loss. However, when a pursuit is lost, the Postmortem evaluates the RDS approach and the resource team's accuracy in executing their plan. Hindsight is 20/20. Use the postmortem as a learning opportunity to increase the chances of successes by capitalizing on team challenges that teach resources to have 20/20 vision in the heat of a pursuit.

Conducting a Postmortem

1) Within 24 hours of learning that a new and/or existing customer has decided not to buy from you, assemble all key resources who played a role and conduct a Postmortem on what went wrong, why and what you learned.

2) Schedule a team conference call or meeting to discuss the following:

- What specifically cost us the business? List the quantifiable reasons both stated and implied.
- Review the pipeline, brainstorming activities, decision mapping and call plans to determine what the resource team really knew, thought they knew and didn't know. If there was no written plan or decision map, that was your first mistake.
- Did we correctly categorized the customer as a high or low probability?
- Reflecting on all interactions with the prospect, what clues should have indicated the resource team was not going to get or keep the business?
- What were the specific dates, conversations and/or meetings when we should have put the clues together in an unbiased way?
- Did we follow all aspects of the RDS methodology or take short cuts?
- Did we properly plan and balance resources?

> **Conducting a Postmortem (cont.)**
>
> • Did we create the right questions for the right players in the decision-making process and establish solid call plans?
> • Did we follow up/follow through to correctly understand their decision-making process and the Buyer's Stage of Buying?
> • Were all issues and potential blockers revealed and addressed correctly?
> • Did the team honestly listen or did we hear what we wanted to hear?
> • Did the team accurately anticipate and negative plan for most possible situations based on the team's research and available data?
> • Was the competition a better value? Why or why not?
> • Was the competition better connected to the people making or influencing the decision?
> • What should each resource have said or done differently now that you know what you know?

A Postmortem is an objective critique of the RDS methodology, not a criticism or condemnations of the individual resources involved in the approach.

Unless something is completely undetectable, or the customer lies and deceives the team, there should be a clearly identifiable reason for how and when the team failed to earn the customer's trust and business.

Even if the customer lied or deceived the team, or if something undetectable derailed the resources, RDS should uncover it. A Postmortem is an objective critique of the RDS methodology, not a criticism or condemnations of the individual resources involved in the approach. Individuals can and will fail to follow RDS, but the approach itself does not affix blame on any individual resource. The responsibility for all errors lies with RDS itself because

challenging each other to follow RDS is the responsibility of the entire resource team. Failure of any kind is shared, but the culpability lies with whether RDS was properly executed or not. As long as the team agrees that they will learn from mistakes and build those lessons back into RDS, they begin to eliminate the potential of the same errors occurring again. Most of our clients find their first Postmortem session scary, even painful and embarrassing. However, the feedback we receive after a Postmortem is conducted is astonishing. The value the Postmortem brings to refinement of the overall RDS application, without focusing or assessing blame on individuals encourages nearly everyone to participate. Subsequent Postmortems are not only requested, the resources actually welcome them and view them as a valuable educational element of RDS. Never placing blame on the resources involved, even when RDS doesn't succeed the first time, Postmortems remove the element of failure for the individuals involved, ensuring their level of comfort and participation in future pursuits.

Today, this approach is rare in most traditional sales organizations. Fear of retribution can lead to a finger-pointing blame game and even worse, it can stifle essential creativity and risk taking. Finger-pointing is very much alive and prospering throughout the hallways of corporate America. When a sales team or individual fails to secure or keep a customer, somebody usually receives the blame.

> *Finger pointing is very much alive and prospering throughout the hallways of corporate America.*

Many times, management will blame the salesperson, who in turn may blame someone else. Blaming uncovers the natural instinct in people to fight for survival as well as the desire to minimize the possibility of ever finding themselves in a similar situation again. Survival tends to take the form of finger-pointing, offering temporary relief to the individual, but it will not foster trust, teamwork and solidarity within an organization. It should be no mystery why most organizations place a wedge between sales and operations functions, thinking "whenever possible, steer clear of selling, prospecting and customers in general," which just reinforces the fear of failure, discouraging participation in growth and retention efforts.

Chapter 13 Highlights

1. The third Epiphany, *Remove the Possibility of Failure, Even When RDS Itself Fails*, resulted in the creation of the 10th and final Core Element, the *Postmortem*.
2. The Postmortem is an objective critique of RDS, not the people involved. Errors in accurately collecting, categorizing and interpreting the fact from the customer's viewpoint are identified and assessed in RDS itself.
3. The Postmortem removes the last possible chance that a non-sales resource can fail when participating in RDS, encouraging more participation from non-sales resources, the fuel that powers RDS.
4. Customer retention is the main component in successful new customer growth.

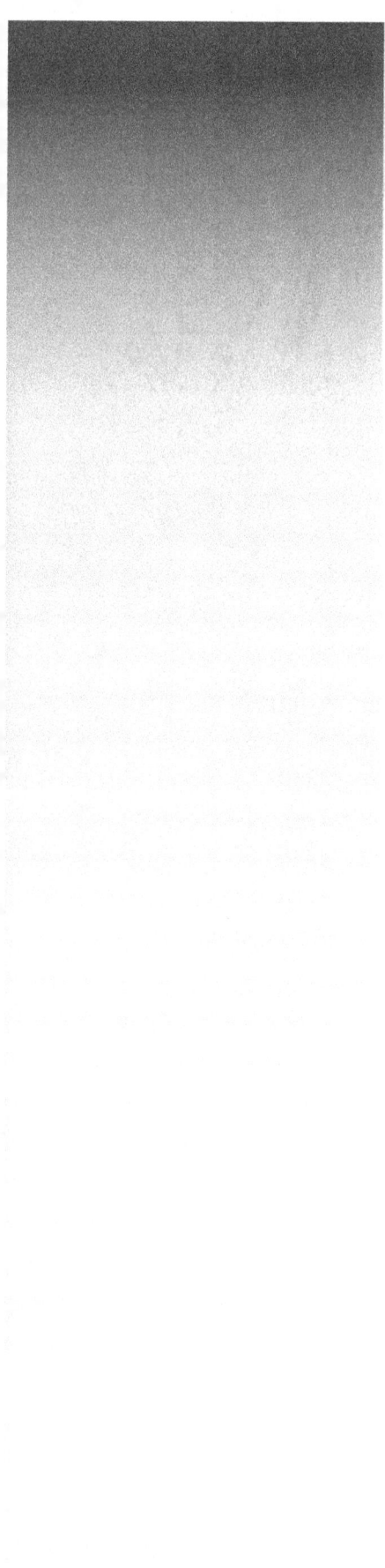

Chapter 14 Prospecting Made Easy

CHAPTER SNAPSHOT
- Prospecting should be everyone's responsibility.
- Minimizing the risk of failure by focusing on quickly getting to "Yes" or "No" encourages greater resource participation.

The building blocks that can help establish the foundation for resource involvement in RDS have been explained. Reducing the fear of failure by minimizing the risks associated with prospecting and retaining customers are essential in encouraging blended resource involvement, trust and confidence. This chapter provides a little extra boost of confidence for resources who only have occasional customer interactions. With RDS, prospecting for new opportunities is everyone's responsibility. From the receptionist to the CEO, everyone is considered a resource, and every resource represents the team and the company. Those RDS resources who take a part-time role in prospecting often ask for the short version of how to prospect for new customers. We provided guidance to a highly technical product consultant who did not have or even want selling experience, yet in less than two weeks, she qualified her first prospective customer. She went on with members of her resource team to actually secure a contract for over $1 million. *PROSPECTING: Quickly Get to YES or NO* lays out the steps she followed to qualify and ultimately secure a customer.

> *From the receptionist to the CEO, everyone is considered a resource, and every resource represents the team and the company.*

PROSPECTING: Quickly Getting to YES or NO

SET EXPECTATIONS

1. You are not asking for or selling anything
2. Don't use brochures, presentations or sales pitches
3. Success = YES or NO

Choose a prospective customer (from the pipeline, if you have one)

Ask 1 or 2 questions, specific to your area of expertise and pertinent to the individual you are talking to

State your name and describe your job function, then ask if they have just 3 minutes, or if there is a better time to call back.

"My name is Mary Frank. and I am a billing coordinator at ABC. I have two questions to ask you that will take less than three minutes of your time. Is this a good time, or is there a better time that you'd like me to call you back?"

CREDIBILITY Question

"As someone who lives with the difficulty of dealing with inaccurate invoices everyday, are you completely satisfied with the billing accuracy you are receiving from your current supplier?"

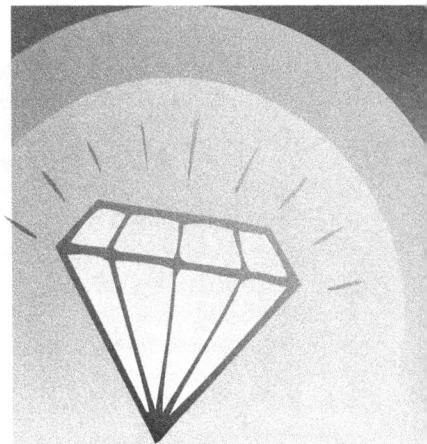

Call, visit or revisit several prospects until you get an *"I'm interested in learning more."*

↑

Ask a parting question such as, *"Would it be OK if I check in from time to time to see if anything changes?"*

↑

Prospect invites you back:
QUALIFIED

- *"When would you like me to call back?"*
- *"Is there anything in particular that you'd like me to be prepared to discuss or share with you?"*
- Schedule discussion with the resource team if necessary

Prospect does NOT invite you back:
DISQUALIFIED

↑

CURIOSITY Question

"I know you are busy, would it make any sense for me or members of our local team to call back some time to discuss what you'd like to see done differently, or do you think you'd rather just leave things the way they are right now?"

↑

Your Reply:
"You know, in this industry that's not uncommon at all, in fact, at ABC we're not perfect either, but we've been told the way we resolve our issues makes us different."

↑

Prospect Responds:
"Yes." "Completely satisfied."

Prospect Responds:
"No." "Not really." "It could be better."

> *Trust is difficult to achieve without constant interaction.*

Some skeptics say this type of prospecting will not work for them because prospecting is a Catch-22. First, they need to be able to get prospects to open up and share their needs, but prospects do not open up and share until they trust and know someone. Trust is difficult to achieve without constant interaction. That is a Catch-22 and it also is a harsh reality today. Therefore, if success seems limited, and there is nothing what-so-ever to lose, we suggest researching the target industry, company and individual and come up with just two very direct closed ended questions that require a "yes" or "no" answer only, nothing more.

Ask a **CREDIBILITY** question: The first credibility question should not be about the individual resource team member, his company or their products, but one that demonstrates to the customer that their business issues are truly understood. A question such as "Does the industry's turbulent pricing practices negatively impact your ability to control and accurately forecast your costs?" indicates that the resource not only knows the buyer's business, but he or she also understands the impact these credibility issues have on the business. If this question hits its mark, the prospect will see the resource as someone that might be different, that might actually understand his needs and therefore someone he may invite back for additional discussions.

Ask a **CURIOSITY** question: The next question to ask

should be a well planned, closed-ended question specifically designed to spark curiosity in the prospect. Hopefully, the buyer already thinks the resource knows more than the typical salesperson, and the well-planned curiosity question will ensure that the resource is invited back for more discussion. We know that if the buyer invites the seller back for additional discussion, the buyer is quite possibly buying or at least in some stage of the Buyer's Stages of Buying. The great news is if he is buying, the seller is not selling! A possible curiosity question might be, "Would you have any interest in learning how several other's in your industry have been able to minimize the pricing peaks and valleys, and therefore they more accurately control and project their costs?" The goal is simply to select the right credibility and curiosity questions to motivate or inspire the buyer to want to invite you back for more dialogue. If the buyer wants immediate information, he is buying; curiosity is piqued, and the seller may have credibility in his eyes. However, the resource is not selling, and shouldn't fall into the trap of making pitches or even talking about the seller's company or its solutions.

Notice that neither the credibility or curiosity question mentions a product or company. They are generic and are not designed to promote anything. If the buyer signals they are buying, continue to create curiosity by suggesting a follow-up meeting at another time after you are able to

> *The goal is simply to select the right credibility and curiosity questions to motivate or inspire the buyer to want to invite you back for more dialogue.*

prepare and plan with the resource team. Refusal to sell will further differentiate the seller and create even more customer curiosity as well as begin to establish trust, which will keep the buyer buying.

Chapter 15 — Tying It All Together

If you still feel that you or your organization will not be able to establish and execute a resource-driven approach based on what you've read, don't worry and keep reading because this is where the pieces come together.

If you are excited by what you have read so far and eager to try resource-driven selling, please put thoughts of designing and implementing your own approach on hold until we can provide you with some final guidance. Consider how you will introduce this type of approach to your organization. Behavioral styles suggest that each person will process, filter and react differently, each requiring a distinctive approach, so plan to adapt to each style. Consider providing as much advance written and verbal information and welcome involvement, questions and suggestions to provide an open forum to all styles, even those who don't like change.

In order to launch and immediately benefit from a resource-driven methodology, begin by adjusting your mindset. Change your frame of mind to involve as many cross-functional resources as possible with your customers. Once that adjustment is made, your organization will be better positioned to implement Core Elements. A resource-driven methodology roll out does not require

> *A resource-driven methodology roll out does not require highly complex or disruptive procedures, but it does involve change.*

highly complex or disruptive procedures, but is does involve change. Change is difficult and takes time for most people, especially if it involves a sweeping adjustment of what has always been done. Don't worry, because quick or complete implementation of a resource-driven approach in the first year is not necessary in order to achieve significant results right away. Designing and implementing your own resource-driven methodology can only occur if a majority of the resources believe in it and brainstorm how they want to establish and drive their own resource-driven approach. To start, just ask for an understanding that something different is on the horizon and the first step will be to involve all resources in the business of growing and maintaining customers.

In Chapter 2 we pointed out similarities between RDS and William Edwards Deming's Statistical Process Control (SPC) because both dramatically changed the status quo. Another common element the two approaches share is that in order to realize a benefit, both begin by implementing in stages. A resource-driven approach actually can provide immediate results once initiated although it starts with fundamental, small steps for buy-in. The full potential of both RDS & SPC is realized over time by applying, learning and continuously applying and improving what was previously learned. However, just starting a resource-driven approach can open the door to both significant learning

and necessary change, including improvements in morale, customer service, reductions in sales and service costs and increased customer retention and growth. Once launched, the initial "pilot" not only paves the way for future expansion and improvement, it also pays for itself.

If your organization takes the first step and involves cross-functional resources in a resource-driven launch, those resources will evolve into more efficient and effective communicators over time. Once management makes the commitment to involve blended resource teams in finding and maintaining customers, the resources should embrace the change in their responsibilities, and as confidence is gained, a resource-driven approach will have been launched and a new mindset will begin to take root.

As I made clear earlier in the book, I was not the most academically successful student. This was obviously not due to a lack of intelligence, although that point may be disputable. Rather, it was because I did not want to adjust to a system I did not like. I finally adapted to it halfway through college, perhaps an indication I am an extremely slow learner! In grade school and high school the only way I thought I could pass tests was to memorize what I thought would be on the test. That approach, when blended with diabolical nuns designing questions that actually required reading the textbook, resulted in a 50/50 chance of me

> *Once launched, the initial 'pilot' not only paves the way for future expansion and improvement, it also pays for itself.*

having the correct answers on the day of the test. That alone should explain my poor grades. But more importantly, that approach explains why I didn't retain much from my early education (perhaps the fact that I was usually doing something to fluster the nuns played a role as well). In college I finally beat the system by understanding the subject matter, not by trying to guess what needed to be memorized. Some step-by-step how-to books propose that following or even memorizing their steps will bring success. However, if you take what we've covered and logically understand the 10 Core Elements and the three Epiphanies, you should take away more than any "Sales for Dummies" instruction can provide.

Launching a Resource-Driven Selling Methodology

Consumers don't make purchasing decisions on big-ticket products and services the way they did 10 or 15 years ago, nor do businesses. To improve an organization's morale, customer retention, growth and customer satisfaction, involve resources in planning and delivering solutions to your customer's problems.

Invite blended resources from appropriate departments to read this book. Brainstorm as a team how your organization can Negative Plan for Positive Results. Encourage input and reinforce that no one is being asked to a become salesperson. As a team, shore up tasks and relationships so if or when old-style salespeople are removed from customer relationships, no negative impact is realized. Consider the guidelines on the next page when establishing a resource-driven selling approach. Make the decision today to implement resource-driven selling, with a blended team of subject matter experts because that's the way buyers want to buy!

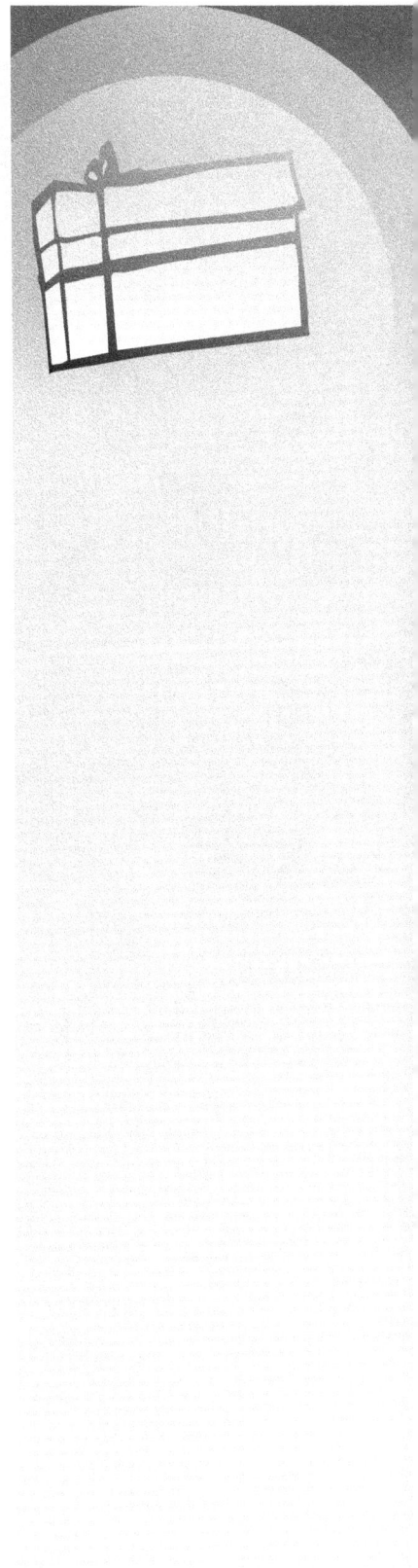

Summary

Resource-Driven Selling Guidelines

1. Involve as many cross-functional, resources as possible and minimize involvement from uncooperative, old-style salespeople.

2. Create customer trust by approaching everything from their viewpoint. Genuinely help to solve customer's problems by involving the entire resource team.

3. Brainstorm, challenge and ensure that resources KNOW the issues, concerns and needs of each individual in the decision-making process by designing effective questions from the customer's viewpoint and behavioral style (DISC).

4. Do everything possible to minimize the possibility of failure. Non-sales, cross-functional resources will confidently solve customer problems and build trust when the possibility of failing is removed.

5. Don't expect anyone to sell, tell or make statements. Honestly help the buyer to buy through well-planned questions.

6. The Core Elements and Epiphanies can be counter-intuitive to what is generally accepted and what most people feel communicating and selling is all about. Don't let naysayers discourage or take the team off track. Be patient, listen and openly discuss RDS because change can be very difficult for many people.

7. The 10 Core Elements are are a blend of good habits and positive communication skills; the Epiphanies showcase negative situations to avoid. However, the knowledge of these negatives can provide positive outcomes.

8. The fear of failure is the main reason non-sales resources avoid customer communication. Review the three Epiphanies and 10 Core Elements, brainstorming with the resource team how to form the foundation of a new resource-driven mindset in your organization.

All three Epiphanies are linked. The first details the seven bad habits that if not eliminated, will prevent the RDS Core Element items from succeeding. The second epiphany embraces pending failure, something typically viewed as a negative. This negative reality can release courage and confidence in the resource team, provoking intrigue on the part of customers. The last Epiphany removes the possibility of failure for any individual resource, by allowing for a look in the rearview mirror by all involved. The Epiphanies remove bad habits and pave the way for new, effective Core Element habits.

EPIPHANY 1

Remove The 7 Deadly Sales Traps

Eliminating the following seven bad habits reduces the risk of failure and increases the likelihood of success.

1. Relationship selling.

2. Selling, presenting and promoting one's product or service.

3. Pitching one's value or solution when the customer voices a need.

4. Approaching from a perspective other than the customer's.

5. Drawing conclusions based on gut instinct or what one thinks, not what one knows to be a fact as specifically related by the customer.

6. Closing, telling and/or issuing price proposals.

7. Confident, experienced salespeople "Winging it" rather than planning and Negative Planning from the customer's viewpoint.

EPIPHANY
2

Redirect Fear to Inspire Risk-Taking and Courage

When there is a feeling that there is nothing left to lose, combining courage with basic survival instincts is intuitively more effective than conservative or politically correct actions and reactions.

EPIPHANY
3

Remove the Possibility of Failure, Even If RDS Itself Fails

Conducting a Postmortem after a failed pursuit reinforces the resource team's confidence that they can prevail in the future by reviewing and pinpointing the actions that were either improperly executed or ignored altogether.

CORE ELEMENT 1

Embrace Negative Planning for Positive Results

Negative Planning exposes and minimizes the risk for failure by concentrating on what can go wrong before anything actually goes wrong. Anticipating the worst from a buyer's viewpoint (what they might say or do) can help prepare a resource team with valuable, proactive, problem solving solutions. Traditional sales approaches focus on the positive outcomes a salesperson may hope will happen. A can-do sales attitude can be another term for happy ears. Resources with happy ears successfully sell themselves but often fail to understand what it takes to satisfy a customer.

CORE ELEMENT 2

Better Positioning Non-Sales Resources to Satisfy Customer Needs

Selling has been replaced by buying because service and sincerity build trust and trust is essential in a buyer/seller relationship. Non-sales resources can be more credible and effective than old-style salespeople who continue to sell, tell and push products and services. Those who make and deliver the product and/or service to the customer can earn more credibility and trust because they view themselves as problem solvers who create and deliver, not salespeople who make promises.

CORE ELEMENT 3

Assess and Capitalize on Resource Strengths

Everyone has an inner brilliance just waiting to be revealed. A simple behavioral assessment (similar to DISC) will identify those inner skills, strengths and attributes. Blending resource strengths minimizes the individual weaknesses and accomplishes much more than risking personality conflicts by deploying the same person every time.

CORE ELEMENT 4

Create a Simple, One-Page Business Plan Tracker

Involving resources from the bottom up when setting and attaining goals can provide more insight, options and an increased likelihood of success. Jointly develop, track, execute, change and improve the team's tactical one page business plan on a regular basis to more effectively link accountability with the resources best suited to deliver the results.

CORE ELEMENT 5

Utilize Pipelines

Creating a growth pipeline that lists potential customers and a retention pipeline that lists current customers can provide the resource team with the ability to prioritize and manage the field of target prospects and customers more efficiently and consistently. A regular review of each pipeline with appropriate resources keeps customer communication and solving customer problems the priority.

CORE ELEMENT 6

Implement Knowledge Quest and Brainstorming

Concentrate on learning as many facts as possible about the customer and their decision process. Challenge the resource team by categorizing "We Know," "We Think We Know," and "We Don't Know" to differentiate the company. Knowledge Quest brainstorming is a self-teaching challenge that builds confidence and inspires individuals and teams to learn what customers need by questioning and listening.

CORE ELEMENT 7

The Buyer's Stages of Buying

Evaluate Current Level of Satisfaction

⬇

Realize a Need

⬇

Review Options

⬇

Sourcing Decision and Implementation

⬇

Satisfaction After Delivery

RDS has no sales cycle because everything in RDS is measured and guided by the buyer's decision-making process. Start by focusing on the customer's level of satisfaction and end with sustaining the customer's level of satisfaction.

CORE ELEMENT 8

Well-Planned Questions

Because buying has replaced selling, questioning the buyer replaces telling, selling, promoting or presenting to a customer. The most essential aspect of RDS is to understand what it takes to satisfy a buyer. Developing questions, tailored to each individual buyer's behavioral style (DISC) is an art and a science each non-sales resource learns in uncovering and understanding the buyer's needs and earning their trust.

CORE ELEMENT 9

Deep Dive Strategy

A Deep Dive planning sessions utilize behavioral style assessments, business plans and pipeline trackers to create scenarios, strategies and questions based on customer styles and the Buyer's Stage of Buying. A Deep Dive serves as a guide when planning how to utilize resources in preparing, executing and following up on each and every customer communication.

CORE ELEMENT 10

The Postmortem

A Postmortem is a resource team's critique of what went wrong when attempting to secure or maintain a customer. A Postmortem is not a management critique or a review of any of the individual people involved. Errors in accurately collecting, categorizing and interpreting facts from the customer's viewpoint are identified and assessed in a Postmortem. This approach removes the last possible chance that a non-sales resource can fail when participating in a resource-driven approach.

Quick Reference Summary

Probability Scale Measurements

0% –	Unqualified
10% –	Contact made – Building relationship
20% –	Needs assessed and interest established
30% –	Internal champion identified
40% –	Decision-making process, players and behavioral styles identified
50% –	Trust established and player needs identified
60% –	Gained commitments from ALL players
70% –	Price, delivery and/or other terms identified
80% –	Negotiating agreements
90% –	Verbal agreement
100% –	Product/service delivery begins

Chapter 5, Page 95

Knowledge Quest - Sample Questions

1. What does this client produce or what do they do to generate revenue? (Do you know that for a fact? How do you know that as a fact?)
2. Does this client/prospect fit the criteria of our niche?
3. Does this client have a "compelling event" that would trigger the need for our product quality, tolerances or delivery standards?
   a. What is that event?
   b. Do all the decision makers understand that they have this need?
   c. How do you know?
   d. Have you asked every decision maker?
4. Who are the decision makers?
5. Do you know for a fact, and do you have a complete list of all decision makers, influencers, approvers, potential blockers and users of our products and services?

Chapter 8, Page 132

6. What is the decision-making process?
7. Is there one or a few decision makers driving the decision-making process or does there need to be a consensus?
    a. How do you know that?
8. Is there a decision maker who is not on board with the company's current course of action?
9. Is that person influential enough to blackball or completely derail this process at some future point?
10. Who actually makes the decision at our company to source the products and services we purchase?
    a. Is it one person or several?
    b. Do you know that for a fact?
11. If you don't know all those who impact our decision to purchase, how can you be so certain you know everyone involved in purchasing for your customer?
12. Would you feel comfortable helping the purchasing agent arrive at our quantifiable value primarily through questioning (not telling or explaining)?
    a. What about the CFO and finance people?
    b. What about the operations people?
13. What is the client's image of our industry? (Positive or negative? Why?)
14. What is the client's image of us?
    a. Does each decision maker share that opinion?
    b. Do you know that to be a fact? How?
15. Are you comfortable reading and adapting to each decision maker's style, needs and personality?
16. Are you successful?
    a. How do you know for a fact?

17. What is the behavioral style of each individual involved in the decision-making process?
18. What is this company's annual sales in dollars?
19. Are their sales trending up or down?
20. In what stage does the company see itself – Emerging, Rapid Growth, a Market Leader or Sustained Market Leader?
21. Who are their competitors?
22. What are the key performance indicators the client monitors?
23. Why are these important to them? Have you asked them?
24. What are the key risks your client sees for the coming 12 months?
    a. 36 months?
25. What could the possible impact be on the business and executives?
26. (If your client has multiple locations) What percentage of their total cost and profit do they currently receive from each location?
27. How are the executives of the company compensated?
28. Does the executive group share in the savings you generate for them?
29. What drives their behavior?
    a. Do you know this for a fact?
30. What do you really know about your clients, competitors and your own company?
31. Do you know enough about your customer, competition and company to provide facts to support your recommendation to reduce price or give away a service?
32. How do you think your competition would fare if given this same challenge?

Common Selling Styles

Selling for Sport: This irrational group approaches selling and negotiating as a sport and tries to win with the expectation that the customer will at least lose something. Where is the logic in winning at the risk of leaving a customer feeling that they lost?

The Giveaway Artist: This salesperson wants the customer to be so happy that the salesperson argues and negotiates harder within their own company than with their customer. In essence, they "give the store away." This lose/win scenario is just as irrational as the win/lose selling for sport but on the other end of the spectrum. This type of salesperson fails to see that loading up with ecstatic customers and an unhappy or unprofitable employer ultimately leads to disappointment for just about everyone involved.

The Ambassador: This group of sellers acknowledge that acquiring the customer's business must be reasonably profitable to the seller while providing a value to the customer. This style of win/win selling is not only a sound, long term strategy, but one of the cornerstones of RDS.

Chapter 9, Page 149

Elements of a Deep Dive

Brainstorming - "What We Know, What We Think We Know, What We Don't Know"

Decision and Resource Involvement Mapping - Identify all players in the customer's decision-making process and the resource team members responsible for communicating with them.

Call Planning - Strategy, Negative Planning and questioning for a customer communication based on individual behavioral styles and the Buyer's Stage of Buying.

Assess Your True Competition - Identifying the strengths and weaknesses of those the buyer considers as options.

Chapter 11, Page 168

Building a Decision Map

Strive to get factual answers to these questions:

- What is the decision-making process and timeline?
- Who are the approvers and decision makers?
- Who are the users, influencers and recommenders?
- Who are the potential blockers we may encounter?
- What are the DISC behavioral styles of everyone identified?
- What is driving their behaviors and what are their needs, issues and concerns?
- What role will they play in the overall decision?
- Where are they in the Buyer's Stage of Buying?
- What does the resource team need to do to successfully address the needs, issues and concerns for each individual?

Chapter 11, Page 174

Creating a Resource Involvement Map

For each resource:

- List their title and role in your organization
- Determine their DISC behavioral style
- Understand their strengths, value and role in the strategy

Chapter 11, Page 176

Elements of a Call Plan

- Meeting Length
- Purpose
- Objectives
- Questions

Chapter 11, Page 178

The Art and Science of Questioning

Applying the correct type of question:
- Diagnostic
- Issue
- Impact
- Solution

At the right time in the Buyer's Stage of Buying:
- Evaluate Current Level of Satisfaction
- Realize a Need
- Review Options
- Sourcing Decision and Implementation
- Satisfaction After Delivery

While adapting to the individual's DISC style:
- Dominant
- Interactive
- Steady
- Compliant

Chapter 11, Page 181

Conducting a Postmortem

1) Within 24 hours of learning that a new and/or existing customer has decided not to buy from you, assemble all key resources who played a role and conduct a Postmortem on what went wrong, why and what you learned.

2) Schedule a team conference call or meeting to discuss the following:

- What specifically cost us the business? List the quantifiable reasons both stated and implied.

- Review the pipeline, brainstorming activities, decision mapping and call plans to determine what the resource team really knew, thought they knew and didn't know. If there was no written plan or decision map, that was your first mistake.

- Did we correctly categorized the customer as a high or low probability?

- Reflecting on all interactions with the prospect, what clues should have indicated the resource team was not going to get or keep the business?

- What were the specific dates, conversations and/or meetings when we should have put the clues together in an unbiased way?

- Did we follow all aspects of the RDS methodology or take short cuts?

- Did we properly plan and balance resources?

- Did we create the right questions for the right players in the decision-making process and establish solid call plans?

- Did we follow up/follow through to correctly understand their decision-making process and the Buyer's Stage of Buying?

Chapter 13, Page 203

Conducting a Postmortem (Cont.)

- Were all issues and potential blockers revealed and addressed correctly?
- Did the team honestly listen or did we hear what we wanted to hear?
- Did the team accurately anticipate and negative plan for most possible situations based on the team's research and available data?
- Was the competition a better value? Why or why not?
- Was the competition better connected to the people making or influencing the decision?
- What should each resource have said or done differently now that you know what you know?

About the Authors

Tim and Chris Morrison achieved their lifelong dream of starting their own business in 2002 when they launched The Geode Group, a strategic consulting company focused on growing and retaining their client's revenue. Utilizing their diverse business experiences, honesty and a work ethic instilled in them by their hard-working parents, Tim and Chris have taken The Geode Group from concept to reality. Many of their greatest achievements are the result of failure and disappointment, but their determination to follow-through regardless of the odds inspired them to pass on their knowledge to others. Their collective experiences in both publicly and privately held companies, their strategic and tactical strengths and leadership in manufacturing, distribution, high tech and financial industries are the basis for *Selling Without Salespeople*, presented in a down-to-earth style that their clients have come to expect, respect and enjoy.

For questions, comments or more information, please contact us at:

www.sellingwithoutsalespeople.com

www.geodegroup.com

info@geodegroup.com

www.ingramcontent.com/pod-product-compliance
Lightning Source LLC
Chambersburg PA
CBHW051210200326
41519CB00025B/7060